Born in Glasgow and raised c
Kenneth White studied French, German and philosophy at the Universities of Glasgow, Munich and Paris. He was first published in London in the mid-sixties (*The Cold Wind of Dawn*, *Letters from Gourgounel*, *The Most Difficult Area* – all at Jonathan Cape), but broke with the British scene in 1967, settling in the Pyrenees, where he lived in concentrated silence for a while before beginning to publish again, this time in Paris. A whole series of books – narrative, poetry, essays – won not only wide-spread recognition in France, but also some of its most prestigious literary prizes: the Prix Médicis Etranger for his book *La Route bleue*, the Prix Alfred de Vigny for his poetry, the French Academy's Grand Prix du Rayonnement Français and the Prix Roger Caillois for his work as a whole. These books have been translated into several languages. Since his return, via Scotland, to the English-language context in 1989, White's work has been published by Mainstream (Edinburgh): *The Bird Path*, *Handbook for the Diamond Country*, *Travels in the Drifting Dawn*, *The Blue Road*, *Pilgrim of the Void*, and by Polygon (Edinburgh): *On Scottish Ground*, *House of Tides*. From 1983 to 1996, Kenneth White held the Chair of XXth Century Poetics at Paris-Sorbonne. In 1989, he founded the International Institute of Geopoetics, which now has centres in various countries, including Scotland, and he directs its transdisciplinary review, *Cahiers de Géopoétique*. Kenneth White lives at present with his wife Marie-Claude, translator and photographer, on the north coast of Brittany.

Open World

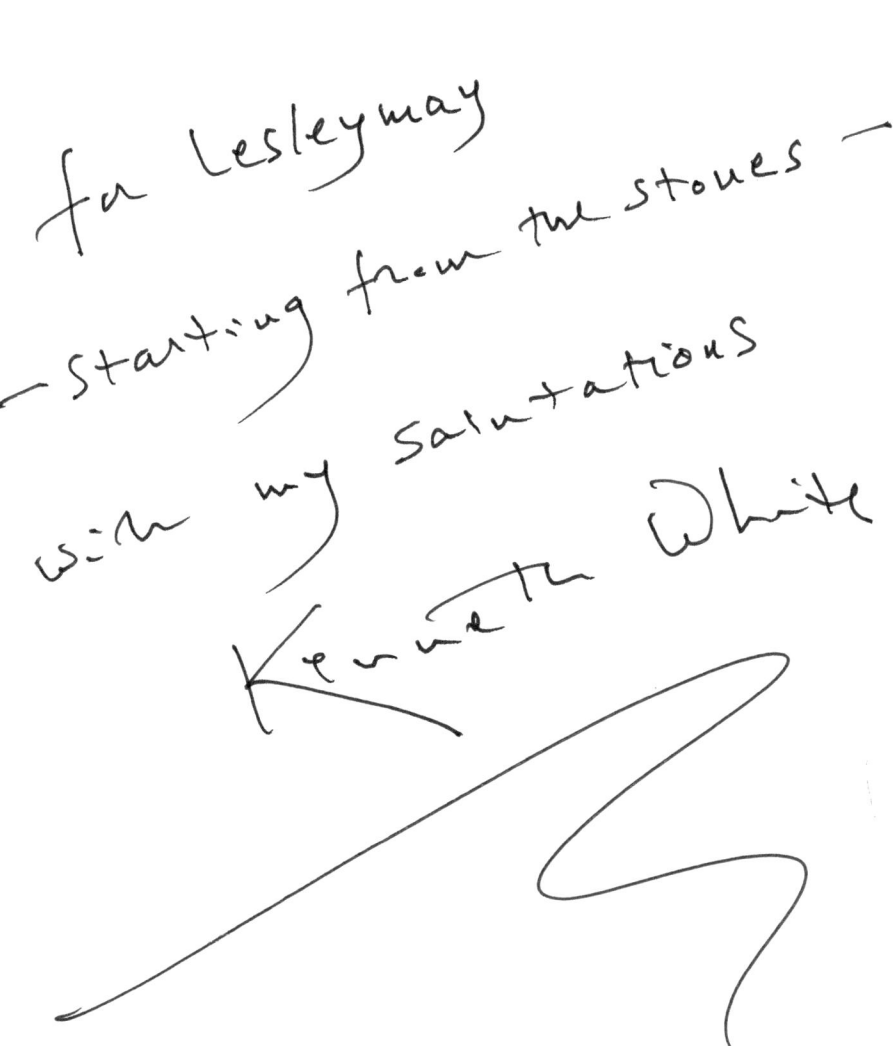

for Lesleymay
— starting from the stones —
with my salutations
Kenneth White

KENNETH WHITE

Open World
The Collected Poems
1960–2000

Polygon

First published in Great Britain in 2003 by Polygon Books

Polygon an imprint of Birlinn Ltd
West Newington House
10 Newington Road
Edinburgh EH9 1QS

Copyright © Kenneth White 2003
Translations from *Atlantica, Terre de Diamant* and *Scènes d'un Monde Flottant* copyright © Editions Grasset & Fasquelle

The moral right of Kenneth White to be identified as the author of this work has been asserted by him in accordance with the Copyright, Designs and Patents Act, 1988

The publisher acknowledges subsidy from the Scottish Arts Council towards the publication of this volume.

British Library Cataloguing in Publication Data

A catalogue record is available on request from the British Library

ISBN 1 904598 01 3

Typeset in Scotch Roman by Koinonia, Manchester
Printed in Great Britain by Antony Rowe Ltd, Chippenham

for Marie-Claude

Contents

Foreword	xxi

Book I : Caledonia Road Blues

Family Alchemy	3
Zone	4
Images of Misty City	5
In the Rain Province	6
Midnight on Atlantic Quay	7
The Winter Lodgings at Scotstoun	8
Pelagius	9
The Wandering Jew	10
Reading Nietzsche on the River Clyde	11
A Dark Secluded Bay in Ireland	12
Heron of the Snows	13
In the Botanic Gardens, Glasgow	14
What Enid Starkie Didn't Know	15
A Letter from my Mother's Father	16
New Moon	17
The Western Gateway	18
In a Café at Largs	19
The Wandering Scot	20
Rue d'Écosse	21
Dunkirk	22
Passing by the University in Glasgow	23
The Ballad of Kali Road	24
On the Border	34
At the Solstice	38

Book II: In the Backlands

Out and down	45
Heraclitus	46
Reconnecting with the River	47
The Strandlooper	48
A Morning in Assynt	49
Dreamground	50
The Ancestors	51
White Valley	52
To the Bone	53
Some Quick Lines from the Eighth Climate	54
Listening to the Wind	55
In the Atlantic Zone	56
Chant	57
Morning Walk	58
When the Frost Came to the Brambles	59
Meister Eckhart	60
Near Winter	61
On the Moor in January	62
Winter Wood	63
The White Hare	64
At the Great Gate	65
The Book at Lismore	66
For MacDiarmid	67
McTaggart	68
Pool Poem for MacCaig	69
Dunbar	70
Happy at Hyères	71
François Villon	72
Three American Beers	73
Pushkin 1837	75
Mandelstam	76
The Study at Culross	77

At Laon	78
Report to Erigena	79
Arthur Schopenhauer in Frankfurt	80
Reading Marpa in the Blue Mountains	81
Tones	82
Stations on the Way	83
Temple near Snowy Mountains	84
Sesshu	85
Kenkô	86
Round North Again	87
A Short Lesson in Gaelic Grammar	88
Carmen Gadelicum 1962	89
Late Autumn on the Findhorn River	90
At St Matthew's Point	91
Black Forest	92
Northern Trail	93
Autobiography	95
The Most Difficult Area	96
Beinn Airidh Charr	97
A High Blue Day on Scalpay	98
My Properties	99
On Rannoch Moor	100
Road Fragment	102
Early Morning Light on Loch Sunart	103
Near Point of Stoer	104
Alba	105
Letter to an Old Calligrapher	106
Rannoch Moor Once More	107
Obscure	108
Into the Whiteness	109
Winter Letter from the Mountain	110
Mountain and Glacier World	111
Late December by the Sound of Jura	112

Rosy Quartz	113
Fossil	114
Theory	115
Example	116
Blue Thistle Sermon	117
Late Summer Journey	118
Ludaig Jetty	119
Beatus	120
Carta Rarissima	121
Letter from Cape Wrath	122
Last Page of a Notebook	123

Book III: Walking the Coast

Sections I to LIII	127

Book IV: The Bird Path

At the Sign of the Rosy Gull	183
Poem to My Coat	185
The Shaman's Way	187
The Gannet Philosophy	192
Tractatus Cosmo-poeticus	195
Letter from Harris	197
The Region of Identity	202
On Bird Island	205
Cryptology of Birds	206
The Bird Path	208
Haiku of the Sud-Express	211
Interpretation of a Twisted Pine	213
Remembering Gourgounel	215
Cape Breton Uplight	217
The Bodhi Notebook	221
River	223
The Wild Swan Scroll	225

Memories of Silver River	226
Scenes of a Floating World	230
Mahāmudrā	235
The House of Insight	240
The Eight Eccentrics	245

Book V: Mountain Meditations

Pyrenean Passage	251
1. To the South-West	251
2. Villa Formosa	252
3. The Tower, 1969	254
4. In the Café of the Reine Marguérite	256
5. Barriers and Passages	257
6. Ossau Valley Notes	259
7. The Flight of Jean-le-Blanc	260
8. Between Two Seas	263
9. Storm at Saint-Jean-de-Luz	265
In Aquitania	266
The Master of the Labyrinth	272
Valley of Birches	275
Crow Meditation Text	279
Mountain Study	283
Hölderlin in Bordeaux	287
Reading Han Shan in the Pyrenees	289
Eleven Views of the Pyrenees	292
In the Sea and Pine Country	294
The Residence of Solitude and Light	298

Book VI: Handbook for the Diamond Country

Another Little Autobiography	303
Culture Telegrams	304
Drinking Green Tea in the Rue St Antoine	305
Archaic Territory	306

The Absolute Body	307
A Fragment of Yellow Silk	308
Intellectual Gathering	309
Gujarati	310
Knowledge Girl	311
Japanee	312
Autumn Departure	313
Crossing the Beauce	314
The Cormorants	315
At Honfleur	316
An Evening at Yvetot	317
The Burgundian Trip	318
On the Plains	319
Message	320
South Roads, Summer	321
Winter Morning Train	322
No Four-Star Hôtel	323
Café du Midi	324
Nameless	325
Avignon	326
Autumn at Meyrueis	327
In the Lozère	328
The White Mistral	329
Fragments of a Red Sea Journal	330
Paradise Lodge	331
Equatorial	332
Turtle Trail	333
In a Bar at Victoria	334
The Insular Contemplations of Pascal Pandanus	335
Philosopher on the Beach	336
The Island without a Name	337
Being, Nothingness and a Bottle of Rum	338
On the African Banks	339

The Afternoon of the Phaetons	340
Sunrise	341
North Station Note	342
At the Red Cloister	343
A Raw Blue Morning in Antwerp	344
The House of Erasmus	345
Letter from Amsterdam	346
The Tower at Tübingen	347
Schopenhauer in Berlin	348
Kant in Königsberg	349
Stockholm	350
In the Blue Tower	351
Strindberg at Lund	352
A Consideration of the Norwegian Sea	353
At the Head of the Fjord	354
Letters from the Lofoten	355
Bergen–Oslo Express	356
Warsaw	357
On the Baltic Coast	358
Black Sea Letter	359
October on Corsica	360
Seneca's Exile	361
A Winter Evening in Bastia	363
Along the Adriatic	364
Vico at Vatolla	365
San Pelagio in the Rain	366
Found on the Shore	367
The Last Days of the Academy	368
Xenophanes of Kolophon	369
Five Little Greek Ones	370
Patmos	371
Europe in the Fall	372
Atlas	373

Bedouin	374
A Morning's Work	375
South-West Corner News	376
The Pinelands	377
Port-de-Richard	378
A Golden Day on the Gulf	379
Equinox	380
Monte Perdido	381
Extraordinary Moment	382
Mountain Study in Winter	383
Rock Crystal	384
In a Mountain Hut	385
Prose for the Col de Marie-Blanque	386
Saturday Night Whisky Talk	387
The Winter-Spring Phase	388
The Road of Light	389
Wakan	390
Misty Mornings in the South-West Studio	391
A Little Epistle from Spain	392
Extremadura	393
Passage West	394
The American Pelican	395
Old Man in Dogtown	396
Somewhere in New England	397
While Reading Robert Frost	398
Letter to Alaska	399
A Snowy Morning in Montreal	400
At Cape Tumult	401
Tadoussac	402
West Labrador	403
Achawakamik	404
Autumn Afternoon	405
Ungava	406

More News from Montreal	407
Point Omega Transit	408
A Short Walk among Primal Signs	410
The Rainy Season on Martinique	411
News from the Islands	412
Quiet Days on Guadeloupe	413
Memories of Indian River	414
Semaphore Hill Soliloquy	415
Another Island Journey	416
The Anegada Passage	417
Seven Views of Virgin Gorda	418
In Praise of Pelicans	420
Companion of the Morning	421
Farewell to an Island	422
Final Note	423
Way Back	424
Eastern Waters Again	425
Autumn at Luk Wu Temple	426
Between Kaifeng and Kweiteh	427
The Lung-Shan Folk	428
A Little Chinese Story	429
In the Mountains of Taiwan	430
Stones of the Cloudy Forest	431
Rangoon Rag	432
Earth Dance	433
Autumn in Kyoto	434
North Road, Japan	435
In the Straits of Tsugaru	436
Joseph Martin's Report	437
Back on the Atlantic Line	438
Settling into Yet Another Place	439
On the Quay at Lannion	440
At Gwenved	441

Somewhere in Brittany	442
The Old Sea-Chapel at Paimpol	443
Ile de Bréhat	444
Goaslagorn	445
Point to Point	446
Armorica	447
Strathclyde	448
Aberdeen: a Pilgrimage	449
A Letter from Wisconsin	450
Good News out of Russia	451
Flotsam	452
Heard on the Moor	453
Autumn at Gwenved	454
On the Promontory	455
Meditant	456
Getting Things Ready for the Guest	457

Book VII: Leaves of an Atlantic Atlas

Venetian Notes	461
Codex Oceanicus	465
Isolario	472
Fragments of a Logbook	476
The Western Gateways	480
In the Sand Parishes	488
The Ocean Way	490
The Armorican Manuscript	493
Broken Ode to White Brittany	501
The House at the Head of the Tide	505
Ovid's Report	509
Brandan's Last Voyage	515
Labrador	520
Logos Amerikanos	526
An Orchestrated Chronicle of the Island	535

The Winter Ceremony	540
Melville at Arrowhead	544
Gauguin in Brittany	546
The Chaoticist Manifesto	550
First Colloquium of the Gull Academy	554
Letter from the Isles of America	559
Elements of the American River System	563
The Northern Archives	565
In the Nachvak Night	567
The Virgins	569
On the Florida Keys	573
Finisterra *or* The Logic of Lannion Bay	575
The Domain of Gwenved	578
Low Tide at Landrellec	580
Lament for McManus	583
The Poetics of Rain	585
Late August on the Coast	588
Scotia Deserta	598
Notes*	603

---

*Throughout the book an asterisk accompanying the title of a poem refers to a note

Foreword

Every world-epoch is marked on its heights by a cosmological (cosmopoetic) idea which creates the field of high endeavour in that age. In ancient Greece, at the height of Athenian culture, it's the idea of *Polis*, or, shall we say, Platonic politics (based on philosophy and science). In the Middle Ages of Europe, it's the Marian Idea – I mean the image of Mary and Child (backed by theology and philosophy). In the Modern Age (dominated by techno-science), it is, with disastrous consequences, the idea of the Mastery of Man over Nature.

It has been the aim of high energy poetics over the last hundred years and more – beyond the Babel of literature and the provinces of restricted poetry – to attain to such an idea (let's say idea-complex, cluster of ideational energy) and create a new field.

The task has been no easy one.

Away at the beginning of the nineteenth century, while he was still close to Hölderlin, Hegel was to say that in the century to come poetry would find itself faced with such an enormous mass of the prosaic (what Mallarmé was to call 'universal reportage') that it would find it difficult to make headway. Later he was to abandon that way altogether (Hölderlin was by this time mad in a tower at Tübingen), declaring that the Idea was latent in History, that History was not only meaningful (not 'a tale full of sound and fury, signifying nothing', as a poet had called it), but gravid with 'World Spirit' (*Weltgeist*). It was this Idea, translated in more popular terms into a Myth of Progress, that carried the nineteenth century along, and a good part of the twentieth. It no longer carries weight at all. Towards the end of the twentieth century, it was entirely blasted, leaving in its wake an anxiety and a vacuum that societies and nations make haste to try and fill up with various brands of 'circus' and 'culture' in the merely sociological sense (anything and everything that is done).

The question remains entire and open.

Throughout history, there have always been individuals that are more lucid, radical and perspectivist than others. Already at the end of the nineteenth century, there were minds absolutely sceptical as to the historical *Weltgeist,* utterly unconvinced that what I like to call 'the Highway of Western Culture' was leading necessarily to something desirable and life-enhancing. I'm thinking principally of Nietzsche and Rimbaud. Nietzsche's 'Eternal Return' is hardly a declaration of faith in the linear conception of Progress, and Rimbaud, looking at that line, was to cry out: why shouldn't it turn? Both are ferociously critical of the culture, thought and art going on around them. Nietzsche's remarks on poets and poetry are, with very few exceptions, scathing. While calling himself 'a poet – at the limit of the word', he tries to create a new figure: that's the *Künstlerphilosoph* (the artist-philosopher) and the *Übermensch* (the post-humanist). Rimbaud rejects most art as foolish and futile. While existing as they can – wandering around Europe and the world – they try to begin again from radical ground. 'If I have any taste for anything at all', said Rimbaud at one point, 'it's for earth and stones' – and the last things he wrote were texts describing the plateau country of Abyssinia. Nietzsche spends his most creative time ('Does any one else in this age know what real inspiration means?') on the plateau of the Engadine, saying: 'Brothers, remain true to the earth.'

I've evoked the wandering life of Nietzsche and Rimbaud. Exodus and exile was going to mark the lives of the principal poet-thinkers of the twentieth century. I'm not talking about political exile – though in some instances this could also be the case: there are political situations and states in which thinking and writing in themselves are considered subversive activities. I'm not talking about 'inner exile', whether that take the form of the eccentric, the Ivory Tower aesthete, or the Bohemian. I'm talking about an exile that is the search for new co-ordinates and regrounding.

Take a case in point, this time in the 'Anglo-Saxon' context: I'm thinking of Ezra Pound. 'Out of key with his time', he is out to 'resuscitate the dead art of poetry'. To do this, he starts off as an aesthete, in a smalltown, self-conscious, imitative kind of way. Thereafter, breaking away from the colleges of Idaho and the drawing-rooms of Bloomsbury, thanks largely to Fenollosa's work on the Chinese ideogram, he begins to conceive of a writing that would be a kind of stenography of the live operations of Nature – as far away as he could get from the solemn metaphysical rhetoric, the emotional outpourings, the rhymed or unrhymed comments on this or that also called 'poetry'. Thereafter, knowing that the function of a powerful poetry is to radiate out into society and ultimately to 'make cosmos', he plunges into the hell and nightmare of history, on the hunt for 'the gristly roots of ideas in action' and moments, models, of coherence and clarity. He gets lost, like so many others of the time, in that historical farrago, saying finally that 'it coheres – even if my notes do not cohere'. What he is left with at the very end, amidst 'a tangle of works unfinished', is 'a little light, like a rushlight, to lead back to splendour', 'a thin trace in high air' and 'bare trees walking on the skyline'.

It's at this point, where I started out, I can begin to allow myself perhaps a more autobiographical approach.

As a British-born poet, I began publishing from what was then the civilisational, cultural and commercial centre-point, London. I published there two books of poems, *The Cold Wind of Dawn* (a very Nietzschean and Rimbaudian title), and *The Most Difficult Area,* that came closer still to a limit (of radical silence), alongside a book of regrounding (both of existence and of literature): *Letters from Gourgounel.* Those three books were considered as anomalies, outside, as one critic put it, 'the muddy eddy of contemporary literature'.

What was 'contemporary literature', poetry included, in Britain? My impression was that, having seen, during the 1939–45 war, that ideas, especially as interpreted by power-crazy, demagogical nitwits such as Adolf Hitler, could lead to terror, disaster and devastation, British Intelligence had come to the conclusion that it was much safer to have no ideas at all. There was little intellectual energy in the air. To speak specifically of poetry, it was what I called 'lawnmower poetry': it hummed and hawed, with functional competency, in a very circumscribed context. One poet asked: 'How dare we now be anything but numb?' Another declared that the extent of his ambition was to 'keep the good old habit alive'. This was to be 'the English tone' for some time, with little additions coming in now and then, from here and there, in the shape of more or less punky populism, hepped-up hymns to speed and violence, or various brands of mythological revivalism. Very little with any ground, scope or perspective.

My own early working references were to Pound – but without his obstinate political aberrations, and with an attempt at more coherence, based maybe more on geography than on history. To Eliot, but not the Eliot established in the academies (classical, royalist, anglican), rather the wanderer in the wasteland who, in his series of 'landscapes' (in particular the one written in New England, on Cape Ann), writes: 'Resign this land at the end, resign it to its true owner, the tough one, the sea-gull – the palaver is finished.' To William Butler Yeats in Ireland who, after looking to a Celtic revival via mythology, had come to the conclusion that there was 'more enterprise in walking naked'. And to MacDiarmid in Scotland – I shared neither his Marxism nor his nationalism, but I valued his attempt to get out of *echtbritische Beschränktheit* via the injection into the poem of great masses of scientific information (what this lacked was selection and shaping), and by his sense of desertified solitude. In America (as a Scot, I felt closer to America than to England), there was William Carlos Williams, re-reading American history (*In the American Grain*), trying to attain to a contemporary coherence (in *Paterson*), and looking towards what he called a 'new leap of the imagination' (which I saw rather as a new leap of the intelligence – poetic intelligence). Also Olson, working ishmaelitically, in the wake of Melville, on the Atlantic edge, at 'a restoration of the human house'.

When I presented my fourth manuscript to my London publisher, I was told that it was 'continental' (in other words, 'not British') and 'fundamental' (in other words, outside the circle of normalised publishing), and was advised to 'put it in the fridge' for ten years and in the meantime establish my reputation by writing a solid novel. What 'a solid novel' meant was exploiting my Glasgow experience in terms of regional social realism, which did not interest me. Another London publisher I went to see at that time made the situation even clearer: he had, he declared, nothing to do with 'culture', he was in 'the entertainment industry'. In other words, the syndrome of the 'best seller', superficially fabricated according to recipe, and the general industry of fast food literature, already well established in the USA, had reached Britain, cluttering up even more, and with more and more noise, the already dingy and trivial socio-cultural scene.

That's when, knowing well that poetry has more to do with the ecstasy journey than with anything like an entertainment industry, I entered into Atopia.

Atopia meant, in the first instance, France. For the next few decades, I was to be in France, and, to some extent, but only to some extent, of France. When I told my first London publisher that I would go to France to further my work, his reply was: 'Ah, but France is a literary country.'

This was true. The line of high literature hadn't yet ended there. Nobody confused literature with whodunnits written by ladies and gentlemen in country towns or universities. But even there, my allegiances and affinities were with poets and writers who were by and large expatriates from any established literary scene, continuing where Rimbaud had left off. André Breton's Surrealism was not concerned with 'literature', but with *magnetic fields*. Alongside Breton, on an energy map of poetic-intellectual France, I'd place Artaud and Michaux. At some distance from this particular constellation, Blaise Cendrars and Saint-John Perse.

Topologically, France had meant for me, and was to continue to mean, alongside Paris, a lone farm in the Ardèche facing the crest of the Tanargue mountain ridge. After my break with Britain in 1967, it meant, from an apartment in Pau, the skyline of the Pyrenees. And since 1983 it has meant an old granite house on the North coast of Brittany, facing the Atlantic.

Atopia ...

For a long time, I felt that all of my writing, whether in prose or in poetry, constituted something like 'the latest news from No Man's Land', a cry in the wilderness.

But this, as I've suggested, is the case with all of the writing in the twentieth century that really means anything, and will continue to mean something, being more than just the spin-off from some local and time-bound psycho-sociological precinct. And from early on, as I'd written in a poem, I'd known the necessity to 'give yourself room for a real beginning' – that is, enter into a large, uncoded space, in order to attain to a greater dimension of one's-self and, *ipso facto*, to a greater work-field.

In that field, I worked at poem, prose and essay. In the poem, without going back to myth, metaphysics or religion, I tried to get out beyond personal poetry and social poetry and linguistic poetry, into what I called 'world poetry', poetry concerned with *world,* that is, what emerges from the contact between the human mind and the matter-energy of the universe. In the prose narratives, out to carry with them more poetic, existential and intellectual energy than the novel, and which I came to call 'way-books', I travelled through territories, culling elements from all the cultures of the known world, moving out from congestion to liberation and a sense of being 'at home in the universe'. In the essays, I worked out neological and neo-logistic notions such as 'atopia', 'supernihilism', 'intellectual nomadism', 'erotic logic', 'chaoticism', 'littorality', 'biocosmo-poetics', and, finally, 'geopoetics'.

Here we move back from autobiography to generality.

I began this 'report' by evoking the necessity, for anything that can be called an *epoch* of civilisation and culture, of a cosmic idea. It was to something like this, with 'biocosmopoetics', 'chaoticism' and 'geopoetics', that I had come in my own work. But I had begun to see also that 'cosmological thought' (not as more space-ships, but as something analogous to the Greek contemplation of the cosmos or the Chinese sense of Tao) had entered into twentieth-century science. It begins with Einstein's *Kosmologische Betrachtungen* of 1917, runs through the theory of general relativity and quantum physics, and attempts to open out on to a new culture-field. The words 'poetry' and 'poetics' turn up again and again in books on scientific thought. So many scientists begin to try and write 'poetically'. The result is more often than not various types of logorrhea rather than anything like a new *logos* (a new co-activation of *eros, logos* and *cosmos),* but what counts here is the desire. Something analogous has taken place in biology. Not only is the development of the organism described in terms of 'auto-poetics', but the conception of the human being as an 'open system' leads to the idea of a language common to mankind and the universe. We can see a similar expansion taking place in philosophy. When Heidegger wishes to renew, reground philosophy, trying to get at 'original areas' philosophy has never heard of, it is eminently to poets, such as Hölderlin and Rilke, that he looks.

In other words, if geopoetics, following on from biocosmopoetics as being simpler and more concentrated ('the making of a world'), had seemed to me a useful word to describe the field into which my own work had entered, it also seemed a useful word to describe a potential general field.

In fact, it is possible that poetics, from having been relegated, in Modernity, to a secondary status, may once again be seen for what it potentially is: an activity that is primal for any live and enduring culture.

Work in progress.

What was horizon in the twentieth century may, in the twenty- first, turn into a field of world-culture. But then, on the other hand, so strong are the forces of massive indoctrination, indeed cretinisation, it may not. Whatever be the historical situation, and the date on the calendar, I trust the great workfield will continue, here and there.

K. W.
North coast of Brittany
July 2003

BOOK I

Caledonia Road Blues

Beginnings. Big city din: dock hammerings, river horns, station whistles – with bits of threepenny opera, Scotch-Irish folksong and blue jazz drifting in through the rain. Street stravaigings. Genealogies. Ecstatic studies in cold rooms. An overall atmosphere of desperate but hilarious supernihilism.

Family Alchemy

When I think of them all:

a dancing rascal
a red-bearded fisherman
a red-flag-waver
a red-eyed scholar
a drunken motherfucker...

I take a look in the mirror
and I wonder.

Zone

Sun a beetroot thrown in mud
six o'clock winter in Dumbarton Road

oatcakes and milk I buy at the dairy
as cars spit their way towards the ferry

the lampstands caught in beginning frost
send out whiskers of light that are lost

in the electric bonfires of the passing trams
while bored-looking women lug their prams

to family tea. I could go home at once and eat
but I wait till the rush is over in the street

and feel that deep loneliness cover my mind
now the moon has appeared like a turnip rind

above the cranes and the gables. The Caspar Hauser song
trails in my conscience as I trudge along

stopping at the corner to drink the milk
while a cat spick and span in genteel silk

black and with inaccessible eyes surveys with disdain
my enterprise decides he need not remain

and slips off into a close without a backward look
I think I shall make an excursion to Pollok

for I cannot return to my spurious home
where all day I've written of Jonah's tomb

I shall take my trip on the trams and hope
that my spirits will be not too ashamed to elope

with the first image tossed from the city's rusty womb.

Images of Misty City

1.
Betty's Bar the Ship Inn
Dick's Bar the Dublin Vaults

Saturday night, the Broomielaw

pink 'papers fluttering at the corners
like exotic birds.

2.
Queen's Dock on a Sunday morning
a noisy bevy of drunken gulls

the pier lined with pungent barrels
of sourmash bourbon whiskey

from Louisville, Kentucky, U.S.A.

3.
Thick fog over the docks
and as thick a silence

only one name of a ship
lit by green light

Sunrana, Kristiansand.

(Writ in The White Tower, tearoom, Glasgow)

In the Rain Province

It's a dark mauve welt
across the map of Europe
the Province of the Autumn Rains

here in the territory
this October Saturday morning
at the top of Byres Road
(where the Byres hit the Great Western highway)

it's a drifting grey drizzle
and a scattered flight of blue pigeons.

Midnight on Atlantic Quay

In the world there is fog
>   and rain
>   and mud
>   and grease
>   and stench

that's the cargo that Glasgow
unloads on my mind
and tonight it's all there:
>   the fog
>   the rain
>   the mud
>   the grease
>   the stench

while I improvise a lonely blues
to which the boats contribute
boat that comes up the river
boat that goes down the river
fog-horns in action
the one sounding: *glas*
the other: *gow*
 as though the city
were blowing trombone
ready to jazz with the sea.

The Winter Lodgings at Scotstoun

About to draw the blinds
I see over the rooftops
and the ten thousand chimneys
with the night-fog
settling down over the city
a dark, red sun.

Pelagius*

Jerome, to get rid of him, polemically
said he was heavy
'with Scotch porridge'

but was there ever, I ask you
a brighter mind
a more diamond being

in all the murky history of knowledge?

The Wandering Jew*

    A medieval miniature in the *Hours* of Anne de Bretagne

Comes out of the white wastes
at four o'clock in the afternoon maybe
some time in the XVth century or eternity
wrapped in a dark-blue cloak of grief
a dog there scowling at his frozen heels

looking for refuge at this French house
where the servants are busy with food and firewood
(what chance has he?) his foot is on the stair

(perhaps they will not know him? have forgotten?
it is so long ago: it would be good to stay ...
perhaps this house needs a secretary?) He enters –

next day along the hedges, a blizzard blowing.

Reading Nietzsche on the River Clyde

A room in a poor district
at the top of a staircase
a hundred steps high
in a steep and narrow street

'*Sono contento*' he would say

Genoa: energy and clarity
a gay hard-living people
the mountains and the sea

'There are many dawns'
he had read in the Vedas
'that have not yet shed their light'.

A Dark Secluded Bay in Ireland

Mother of mine for five days now
this heart has been smoking thick black melancholy

the rain is running down every hump
and there's not a bit of yellow sun in sight

I sit scraping away at this deal table
like an old angel trying to learn the fiddle.

Heron of the Snows

        Chinese studies on Maryhill

China, Xth century, when Siu Hi
painted his Heron of the Snows
on a Frost-covered Branch

the ungainly, cold-eyed bird
the mass of white plumage against
the grey sky, the uncouth claws

and Chuang-tzu asked: what
does the great bird see that can rise
so high in the wind? Is it original

matter whirling in a dust of atoms?
the air that gives life to creatures?
the unnamed force that moves the universe?

on the riven branch, the heron
like the ghost of an answer
balances in the wind

and stares at the questioning world.

In the Botanic Gardens, Glasgow*

1. The banana plant, Bashô

He was a poet
out for unheard poetry
and he wanted, badly, a new name
(that was in old Japan
seventeenth century)
then all at once, out of the blue
from that ordinary, plain plant, *bashô*
there it came –
quick as lightning he scrawled ten haiku.

2. The Tibetan poppy

Deep blue, incredibly blue
it grows along the paths
of the ecstasy journey
that can start up any time, anywhere

why not here?

3. Silver birch

It's been at the centre of myth
at the centre of legends
but if you can see where it stands
exactly as it is here now
so silver, so slender, so tall
you'll go away beyond them all.

What Enid Starkie Didn't Know*

The army of the Netherlands had got him there
(the East, at last!)
but now, as a damned deserter
it was time to get out, and fast

at Batavia, down by the harbour
he made hasty but discreet enquiries

a Scotch bark
The Wandering Chief
was ready to set sail for Leith
laden with sugar

'Whit'll be yer name, son?
– Rimbaud, Arthur
but I'd rather not sign the register
– Ach, that'll be nae bother
we'll pit ye doon as Henderson, Alan
naebody'll be any the wiser'

one day later
a new lease of life was given
to the craziest wanderer of French literature.

A Letter from my Mother's Father

New York, 1930

I'm gazing this evening through a dirty window
in Brooklyn, at the Hotel Margarita
the red funnels of the *SS Mauritania*
are rising through the Hudson River fog

the hair of the dog, the hair of the dog

at the Beacon Light Mission in Harlem
you get a good strong mug of coffee
for three cents, on the Lower East Side
you can purchase an inch-thick slice
of black rye bread –
two cents extra for butter

what kind of a crazy character
would sell all the house's furniture
to buy a ticket for this?

another of those giant buildings is growing
tickling the clouds, scraping the sky
tapping the heels of God
(to feel something familiar
I go down to the Fulton Market
and look at the cod)

here in Brooklyn, in the blue mackerel evening
I'm dreaming of the old Broomielaw –
nothing having conquered, gained nothing
at least, well, I came and I saw.

New Moon

These walls have grown sullen, and I
lodged between a dairy and an antique shop
between a station and a library, read
no future, live no present, sick
with a bellyful of memory, my skull
like an old tin can that rattles, yet

the sun will move northwards, rising
in the frozen heavens, and the day
will lengthen. New at the month's
beginning, the moon, on the fifteenth night
being close to earth and very full
will raise the tides like whales along the coast.

The Western Gateway

The way out, hah – that blue-
black glower along the river then
the gold-amber flash then again
the blue-black glower long down the river
(old black tramp there and big
fat-bellied lazy white liner)
and fast cloud hung down low
over the greyblack waves with grist-
ling crests (oh the curving fall) above
them blackwinged sheer-flighted gulls

And the hills then, red fern entang-
lements and thorn and wild rose and
holy-red holly among the snow and
the trees stark hung with water –
walking there over blue-ice paths the
streams rushing air driving sharp
and that light crazy-clear that
savage angelic and cosmo-demential light
that shows up the world in its nakedness
swift-changing darkly-bright realness.

In a Café at Largs*

In memoriam Ezra Pound

Blue morning
sea like glass
gulls

'came Neptunus
    his mind leaping
        like dolphins'

the little Filipino waitress
brings me another cup of coffee
with a smile on the side

'these concepts
the human mind has attained'

and the others – still
to be attained.

The Wandering Scot

Scotus vagans

It was a clear, cool, April-blue afternoon
just after the winter snows

I was waiting at a Paris railway station
on a train bound for Aurillac
(the 'place of the winds'?)
up there on France's central plateaux

why the hell go to Aurillac –
God only knows

in my rucksack
(graced with the claw of a grouse)
I had *Sartor Resartus*
alongside an empty notebook.

Rue d'Écosse

> Hill of Sainte-Geneviève, Paris

There's nothing much in the rue d'Écosse
that dark little cul-de-sac –
just the full moon and a stray cat.

Dunkirk

Sea vespers

This evening, mid-November
after dinner at the Zanzi Bar
I'm standing at the window of my chamber
looking down over there
at the quiet side quarter
known as Malo-de-la-Mer

watching a light-tower
poke a smudgy finger
from the smoky huddle of Dunkirk
into the Noordzee dark.

Passing by the University in Glasgow*

'Where' cried the Ivory Gull
'where will they find it now
une forme sienne une forme maîtresse'
skimming low over Fidra in April
('maybe in the Study at Culross'
said the Long Ghost 'or maybe
at St Andrews by that tower and window
or maybe on any island')

'And where are the *beaulx livres*
the *beaulx livres de haulte graisse*'
cried a fat rabelaisian Laughing Gull
dropping skite over University Avenue
('maybe in the Canongate' said the Long Ghost
'maybe in the Gorbals
maybe even, God knows, in Aberdeen
anywhere a soul has richly ripened')

'And where' cried the Rosy Gull
le cerveau ivre d'une gloire confuse
'where are the words both complex and simple
saying actual relations to the universe'
('maybe where the tree stands on the moor'
said the Long Ghost 'where the rock
has its hold in the sea, anywhere
that highest intellect meets wildest nature')

'Where' cried the gulls 'where'
                    'maybe' said the ghost.

The Ballad of Kali Road*

A sociocultural extravaganza for several voices,
a tin whistle, a Jew's harp and a sense of supernihilism.

1.
Coming through the Saltmarket
with the powerful stench of fish in my nostrils
past the pub where the old man's old man
earned a few extra shekels
over the Albert Bridge
and the Clyde's turgid waters
this Saturday morning in October
under a pale blue Indian-summer sky
into what remains of the old South Side:
a few gutted redstone tenements
windows smashed, rubble in the closes –
along the new Crown Street
up to the Gushetfaulds
where Dixon's Blazes, roaring and rumbling
used to cast its lurid glare on the sky
the local image of hell
('if ye don't behave yersel
ye'll get sent tae the Blazes!')
now replaced by a couthy carpet factory
about as inspiring as the *People's Friend*.

2.
Don't worry, pal – this won't be a sob-song for *No Mean City* or a remake of *Miracle in the Gorbals*. The old hell-holes no doubt had to go. And they're well and truly gone. We'll waste no time in lamentation. What follows is more in the nature of an invitation to the dance. A supernihilistic dance on this cremation-ground the XXth Century has so conveniently provided for us.

3.
Dancing's always
been in the family
the old man's old man
was a piper and dancer
that is, a Hielant dancer
though he wisnae a teuchter
the old man himself
was hot on the jiggin'
used to shuffle along Florence Street
as one of the Bowler Brigade
used to follow the band
in which his brother played the sax
and would do a bit of singing too
like 'The Birth of the Blues'

but my dance here as you'll gather
is a different kind of thing altogether
having damn all to do
with Highland Reels or 'Stormy Weather'.

4.
I'm what you might call a transcendental Scot.

5.
'Here's tae the good old whisky
drink it down, down, down,
here's tae the good old whisky
drink it down, down, down
here's tae the good old whisky
makes you feel so frisky
here's tae the good old whisky
drink it down, down, down' –
Danny Reilly used to sing that song.

6.
I'm in a pub called Dixon's Blazes
which didn't exist when Dixon's existed
(those were the days of the Hi Hi,
The Rising Sun and 'roon the coarner')
standing all alone in its glory
and cashing in on the old mythology –
because myths won't grow here any more
we're making it on a re-al-ist-ic floor.

7.
Around 1923 in this quarter
my father was collecting rents
for a firm in Bath Street
and was known as 'the wee factor'
but not liking to dun poor folk
he gave up that 'job with a future'
and joined the railway
first on the Carriages and Wagons Staff
then in the signalcabin at Polmadie
where he read Bakunin, Marx, Keir Hardie.

8.
Song about the uselessness of life

We were brought up hale and hearty
though our mother's breast was clarty
and a whisky dribble sometimes touched our lips
we were dragged up by the ears
through a maze of ragged years
and our staff of life was Tally fish and chips

When the nation came to call us
we were fourteen and quite gallus

and we thought the future held the promised land
but the City quickly taught us
that a man's own work and thought is
what the sparrow's to the eagle, to the mighty ocean, sand

We were there to aid production
meant to work without objection
and the prize they held before us was: a wage
just to keep ourselves alive
so the happy few might thrive
and eat the cake of righteousness within their gilded cage

So the slaved enslave the slaves
since we first dwelt in the caves
and society's a hellish rigmarole
you may think that the Creator
planned it all when on the batter
and may turn your arse sky-blue for the saving of your soul

You may try to get together
call the other man your brother
and the venture may seem hopeful for a spell
you may form associations
you may draw up regulations
but your brother's son will twist them all to hell

About the problem that remains
we have often beat our brains:
is it worthwhile hanging on then after all?
there must be some solution
to society's pollution
if you find it, don't forget to give the call.

9.
'Eech harum darum doo
eech harum darum dorus
a think we should aa be shot
for singin' such a rotten chorus!'

10.
A voice from the direction of the Old Wynd Kirk:
'This age also is advancing. Its very unrest, its ceaseless activity, its discontent contains matter of promise. Knowledge, education are opening the eyes of the humblest, are increasing the number of thinking minds ... There is a deepening struggle in the whole fabric of society; a boundless, grinding collision of the New with the Old ...'

Thomas Carlyle, *Signs of the Times*, 1829

11.
To return to the present.
Cathcart Road, October 10th, 1961

'A waant ma hole
a waant ma hole
a waant ma hole-idays
tae see the cunt
tae see the cunt
tae see the cunt-ery
fu'cu—
fu'cu—
fu'curiosity.'

12.
Western culture's oot the windae
(pattin' peas at its blin' auntie) –
bring on the Dancing Girl!

'Because you love the burning ground
I have made a burning ground of my heart
so that you, Dark One
may enter in and dance
the eternal dance
nothing else is in my heart
o Mother Kali
day and night, night and day
the funeral pyre blazes
and the ashes of the dead
are scattered all around
o Kali
enter in and dance
the rhythmic dance
and I shall watch
with closed eyes.'

13.
The old man's old man as aforesaid
was piper, dancer, and publican
also sodger
of the kind that had lice in their kilts
at Passchendaele and Ypres
his wife was the daughter
of a tea merchant from Inverness
and they all lived together
(there were two boays and two lassies)
at No 439 Crown Street
till Tommy left and got mairit
and Nan left and got mairit
and Ellen left and got mairit
and Willie left and got mairit
to Jennie Cameron, daughter of Baldie Cameron

('Baldie' here being short for Archibald
not indicating lack of thatch)
who toiled in a shirt factory in the Shaws.

14.
This hotch-potch might be called: Washing your Dirty Souls in Public, or Dragging the Ghosts from the Closet, or yet again Aa Dressed Up an' Naewhere tae Go.

15.
Jock White wound up with a stroke
and lay paralyzed in his bed
till a minister, faith-healer
came to lay hands on him:
'Do you feel the fluid, John,
are you feeling any the better?'
'Oh, aye, Mr Gillespie,
feelin' an awfa lot better' –
like hell:
when the minister was out the door
his son Willie asked the auld bugger
why he'd lied like that –
'Och, a didny waant tae disappoint the man'
a few days later
he gave one last scunnered look
and his troubles were over.

16.
This was Wee Harry Hope's song:

'A went tae the racecourse last July
far far away
the horse a backed was Kidney Pie
far far away

the horse it won a danced wi' glee
a went tae collect ma LSD
where wis the bookie
where wis he
far far away.'

17.
Where is Jock White? Deid.
Where is Danny Reilly? Deid.
Where is Wee Harry Hope? Deid.
Where is Auld Man Graham? Deid.
Where is Nancy Shaw? Deid.
Where is Sarah Tennant? Deid.
Where is Sam the Jew? Deid.
Where is Seek Peter McGee? Deid.
Where is Tam the Busher? Deid.

– deid, deid, deid
aa that's left is ghost stories.

18.
Song of the Coffin Close

Have you heard of the Coffin Close, boys
have you heard of the Coffin Close
it's one of life's rare joys, boys
it smells like a summer rose
yes, it smells like a summer rose

Have you ever climbed up the stair, boys
have you ever climbed up the stair
where the lavvy-pan overflows, boys
and gives you a whiff of rotten air
yes, a whiff of rotten air

Have you ever fallen down the stair, boys
have you ever fallen down the stair
and buried your sensitive nose, boys
in the filth and muck which is there
yes, the filth and muck which is there

Have you ever come up at night, boys
have you ever come up at night
when the burner throws its rays, boys
you see many a ghastly sight
yes, many a ghastly sight

Have you ever seen Bill McNeice, boys
have you ever seen Bill McNeice
lying dead to the world, boys
and a cat being sick in his face
yes, a cat being sick in his face

Have you ever seen Mary Cape, boys
have you ever seen Mary Cape
she often hangs there on the stairs, boys
coughing her insides up
coughing her insides up

You all know the Coffin Close, boys
you all know the Coffin Close
if I bother you all with my noise, boys
it's all for a very good cause
yes, it's all for a very good cause

I live in the Coffin Close, boys
I live in the Coffin Close
very soon they'll be taking me out, boys
and my head will come after my toes
yes, my head will come after my toes.

19.
Ah, well, Kali
let it all go down the river
on the brown waters
under the empty blue sky
let it all
go down the river
down
down the river
to the long shore
the long white shore
where John Knox
is a hermit crab
and Plato
is a jellyfish.

OM SUNYAJNANA KRIM SVAHA
HERE ENDETH THE BALLAD OF KALI ROAD

On the Border*

An ordinary day in September
in the region of Carter Bar

rough wind, a rock, and a rowan tree

here Scotland begins:
the Scott country
land of daffodil-lawned ruins
and of justified sins
land of the Bible-thumper
with (or without) a sense of humour
land of the inveterate whisky-drinker
and of the predestined golf-player

rough wind, a rock and a rowan tree

the country has lain
for so long under cliché
things have hardly had a chance
to come alive into their own

better by far an Ice Age
quaternary cold
followed by a little clean phenomenology
as when a few thousand years ago
the ice withdrew from the back of these hills
and the Solway Firth started to flow

rough wind, a rock and a rowan tree

let the 'Scottish re-advance' be this
rather than a rehashed renaissance!

but let us avoid polemic
and quietly move over these Cheviots
expanding our brain circuits

thinking of many another border
larger and lonelier

one April day in particular

it was when we topped the rise we saw them:
ten... twenty... seventy vultures
hunched on rocks
hopping in for another morsel of the feed
or running heavily into flight
(the feed, that was
nine sheep and a cat
scattered there
in a heap of blood and fur)
never had I seen so many vultures in those hills
and to complete the rareness of the sight
suddenly
out of the sun
swooped in a *mari-blanque*
circled, carefully circled again
then came in for a bite

we hunched on rocks
about fifty yards from the birds
a face-to-face
in the silence of the mountain
before moving over the frontier into Spain:
that after all is where we came from
before we roamed up into this area
and began to suffer from Anglophobia

let's get back, I suggest, right into the ice
and move out again from there
waving no banner
just putting one foot in front of the other
– that way we're liable to go farther

let's call it
a rediscovery of Alba

cartographies
topologies

the humpy rocks
and the gouged valleys
laid out in their bare lines
slowly colonised
by heather, birch and pines

that old quaternary face
and its archaic expressions
in these border regions

followed by rough stone habitations
animal-raisings
agricultures
depredations

the bitter quarrelling of nations

when you look into the eyes
of the people you meet
in township or in village street
you wonder what worlds
lie behind the bones
what's going on
inside the brain-pans

in the noisy areas:
muzack, politics, T.V. shows
kilts and saddles, buttons and bows

but back of all that
in the silence?

strange minds have grown in this place

it was out of a cow-stream in Ecclefechan
was born the first trans-disciplinarian
('Dr Teufelsdröckh, I presume?')
and it was in these hills Alec Murray
plunging into Salmon's *System of Geography*
got the gist of twenty tongues
– I'm not forgetting either
MacTaggart's *Encyclopedia*
or MacDiarmid's polymathic *poetica*

these Borders border on more than England

the border between nation and nation
is hardly interesting after all
(unless the limit of your ambition
is to write yet another historical novel)
what matters
is the border
between human and inhuman
between one field of knowledge and another
between spirit and matter

Thomas of Ercildoune, here in this place
knew something of that
so did Duns Scot

but today the fields are wider
the forces greater
and we need neither fairies nor Creator

only
in a mind on the edge
a sense of near-infinite space
and of moving, complex reality

rough wind, a rock and a rowan tree.

At the Solstice*

> 'At Christmas, the dead season, when wolves
> live on the wind.'
> (François Villon)

1.
The moon last night was a sheer calamity
a leprous hunchback of a planet
Santa Claus with ice in his sack
had I not gone to bed with the whisky
I'd have surely froze to the floor

as it was, midnight and past
I ascended into the banshee hill
the pipes of winter wildly playing
and the fairy fires of Schiehallion
kindling up my seraphic instinct

they found a lyre in the town of Ur
and its sound-box was a sailing ship
whose figurehead was a bull
two or three millenniums back
this was the instrument I played

I have set my feet in a large room
the nearest thing to the infinite
I am whirling in an orbit of ecstasy
a sudden stirring of matter
and this I call the beginning.

2.
The window's like an arctic map
the gutters are choked with wrinkled ice
the sun is a cheese in a fridge

the seat of my pants is as thin as charity
and my backside has a grudge against the world

I go up to the market to feed my poem
the market women have chappit lips
with red and dribbling noses
four layers of wool around their hips
and smiles like a crack in a mirror

the last will and testament of fowls
is throttled at the source
every bird has goose pimples now
even the turkey that tries to coquet
with a tuft of black plumes in its rump

horse flesh is crimson and grim
shrimps are pink and neat in a box
cockles grin with a salt sea-whiteness
mussels keep their red secret close
and oysters writhe in the cold.

3.
I stand in my own inscrutable whiteness
and my heart is a blazing furnace
and I try to enlarge my soul
and I know that the deepest is the most alive
and I want nothing less than all

I have grown chrysanthemums in the dung of God
I have blacked my boots with the Bible
and walked all over the world
I have lived in the Chinese mountains
and planted bamboo in drizzling rain

to open your eyes and broaden your chest
and take long easy strides

that is the way
to let the holy ghost breathe mountain air
and eat the wild fruits of the earth

for long the world was an inn
an ale-house back of heaven
where all were benighted and lost
but I say the world is a range of possibles
and the flight of wild poems.

4.
Stoke up the fire and light your lamp
never mind the cold and the oncoming dark
take up your books, continue your studies
let no man say you were afraid of the silence
or rotted away in self-pity

animals howl and stare at the moon
take you its force and turn your back
and write in your own whiteness
trace your own progress
all the hidden changes of winter

let the old buzzard snotter and snash
weave the snow to a flannel shirt
with a thick tail to cover your hurdies
use the rain to mix your toddy
and the wind to turn the pages of your book

personal force can work wonders
without it talent is nothing
increase your life
and strengthen your character
make full use of this winter.

5.
From Strathclyde to Whiteness lies the way
through all the wild weathers of the world
and through all the dog-days: *si con Escos*
qui porte sa çavate, de palestiaus sa chape ramendée
deschaus, nus piés, affublez d'une nate

holding the highway, an upland man
singing loud in the barbary tongue
through the winter to the early spring
no false knowledge in the brain
no contrivance in the heart

the hills are still the same remember
and the rivers and the winds
give yourself room for a real beginning
the man who works in a narrow space
builds no more than prison or grave

I wrote this poem in sixty-two
in December, two days from Christmas
my house is secluded and I live alone
but this is the condition of wandering far
and I know I have companions.

(Rue des Basses Pointes, Meudon, outskirts of Paris)

BOOK II

In the Backlands

Going back into the silences. Gathering cold elements. Alban investigations, white world. At the tentative limits. No metaphysical solemnity, no encumbering religiosity. A great emptiness – broken now and then by exclamations, like the cry of a Laughing Gull.

Out and down

Making out of town
to the end of the macadam
where old bracken spreads
darkred in the rain
and thorn grows loosely
in ragged heaps

let me lie here awhile
in the wet and the wilderness
watching
the grey cloud passing
saying a quiet hallo
to a bedraggled sparrow.

Heraclitus

They called him
the dark, the obscure, the mysterious one
o skoteinós

walked the sunburnt rock of Hellas
saying:

'man lives farthest
from what is nearest'

or

'better to put out human fiction
than put out a fire '

nobody got the drift
of what moved his mind

he went from shadow
through blinding clarity
into shadow

o skoteinós.

Reconnecting with the River

>'As I looked me alone
>I saw a river rin ...'
>(Alexander Montgomerie, 16th c.)

A late afternoon in Govan
at the junction of the Clyde and the Kelvin
rain falling on sullen stone

floating on the dark, dank waters
one lone mute swan.

The Strandlooper

Nomad of the coast

paleolithic pathfinder
in the old boreal days

crawled from rock to rock
looking for whelks and limpets
dug for razorfish and cockles

but also spent hour after hour
just wandering along the sands
at nights
looking up at the Great Bear.

A Morning in Assynt

Sitting on a rock in Scotland
thinking of orogenic phases

this is the oldest of the old
older than the ancient caledonian
older by far than the hercynian
or yesterday's alpine

the time of crying crisis is long gone
what remains is a landscape
almost unreadable in its taciturnity

but the red of the heather
goes straight to the heart
and the flight of that white bird
over the ridge
enlightens the mind.

Dreamground

I came in a stranger's guise
over the white pathway, the moon
glared: a glass eye, cold
rain pitted the snow, the firs
on my thought's ragged edge
threw their shadows over mine

a light upshone in a window
see: a robin perched on a twig
amid humps of snow. The bolt
had the touch of a friendly hand
easy and strong, the door watched
between the stove and the elements

I have the warm cup in my hands
and the poker is tuning up the fire
and the dead man I live with
looks at me, questioning
and I search for a word of greeting
in the grammar of moon, rain, snow, and fir

but there is no landscape, and no
language, only a ragged silence
and we sit there face to face
and listen to the falling rain –
blow out the lamp now, let
the stove burn deep in the darkness

uncover yourself to the bone.

The Ancestors

Under grey Harris or quiet Colonsay
the bones of the ancient bards lie weathering

they had their occasions, often making
more than the head man's order might imply

adding that extra twirl, that subtle grace
to details of the bloody chase
or rigmaroles of genealogy.

White Valley

Not much to be seen in this valley
a few lines, a lot of whiteness
we're at the end of the world, or at its beginning
maybe the quaternary ice has just withdrawn

as yet
no life, no living noise
not even a bird, not even a hare
nothing
but the wailing of the wind

yet the mind moves here with ease
advances into the emptiness

breathes

and line after line
something like a universe
lays itself out

without doing too much naming
without breaking the immensity of the silence
discreetly, secretely
someone is saying

here I am, here
I begin.

To the Bone*

Hearing a bird cry

back up there
in the fields behind Fairlie

an autumn afternoon
the air chill
the gold sun turning red

reality right to the bone.

Some Quick Lines from the Eighth Climate

A monk in Scotland, twelfth century

Here we live and toil
beyond the pale
on a little island
surrounded by fitful seas

stark winter
has always been our educator
summertime is short
autumn a long farewell

no paradise
but April, ever a surprise.

Listening to the Wind

1.
Autumn pools on the moors
of brown bitter water

there the cold sun reflects
and shudders when the rain

sweeps down over the hills.

2.
The rotting carcass of a ram
horns creased and gnarled

the pelt heavy and bedraggled
the dip-mark blue on its side

like an October moon.

3.
On the ridge among the stones
and rubble of the abandoned quarry

looking down over at the sea
and the foam-curving islands

listening only to the wind.

In the Atlantic Zone

On Mull
along the Allt na Teanngaidh
among sandstone and schist

on Gunna
with a hundred barnacle geese
ranging along the coast

on Colonsay
lying on a raised beach in the rain
looking out over
a stretch of windswept dune

on Jura
in a cabin near the Paps
gazing on a lump of rosy quartz

on Islay
walking the salty *machair*
that the tide has left
watching out there in the grey
the wan waters of the North Atlantic Drift.

Chant

Birch rites
empty moors
raw skies
incredible snow

mussel beds
gull screams
lost islands
moonglow

wet woods
heron shells
crimson leaves
dark rain

hare pads
lightning flash
written rocks
begin again.

Morning Walk

It was a cold slow-moving mist
clotted round the sun, clinging
to the small white sun, and the earth
was alone and lonely, and a great bird
harshly squawked from the heronry
as the boy walked under the beeches
seeing the broken pale-blue shells
and the moist piles of mouldering leaves.

When the Frost Came to the Brambles

Red they were and black
and the bitter frost
put tang into their sap

I took my breakfast of them
up on the edge of the forest
in mirkness and in mist

old man winter looked down at me
from a ragged fir tree.

Meister Eckhart

Entbildet, überbildet

Born at Hochheim, 1260
studied in city after city

worked hard teaching
talking fast and familiarly
about matters unfamiliar

carried in his head
a vast all-embracing scheme
but only got some of it onto paper:
a couple of telegraphic treatises
here and there a poem

the thing was, as he saw it
to get outside
all limited and cloying images
into an open field of astonishing light

the authorities
understand him not at all
which is why when he died
at Avignon in 1328
he was put beyond the pale

not only erratical but damnably heretical.

Near Winter

Let winter now come

ox-laden sky
cold spume of rivers
nakedness of moors
mist in the forest
let winter now come

the spoor of animals
blue in melting snow
the sun polished hard
birds and berries
bronzen shadow
water icy and thin
black crust of earth
hoar glint of stone
let winter now come

seaweed covers the moon
wind harrows the firth
the islands glint in fog
I fish in cold waters
my boat black as tar
the horned rowlocks
creak to the oar

let winter now come.

On the Moor in January

Moor wind and snow
the roaring of nothingness in my ears
the bite of it on my skin
the craziness that takes hold of me
so I lurch like a madman
and laugh and cry
and lose all proportion

then the tree appears in its grotesquerie
black and twisted, solitary
and I hug it like a brother
more than a brother

rooted unrooted together.

Winter Wood

So I have put away the books
and I watch the last apples fall
from the frosty trees

and I have seen also
acorns stretching red shoots
into the hard soil

and the white bark of the birches
was more to me then than all the pages

and what I read there
bared my heart to the winter sun
and opened my brain to the wind

and suddenly
suddenly in the midst of that winter wood
I knew I had always been there

before the books
as after the books
there will be a winter wood

and my heart will be bare
and my brain open to the wind.

The White Hare

A thought that leaped out like a hare
over the moor, from behind a great rock
oh, it was a white leaping hare, and
the heather was a fine red world
for its joyance, just that day on the moor
a grey day marching on the winds
into winter, a day for a sparkling sea
three miles away in the trough of the islands
a day high up at the end of the year
a silence to break your heart, oh
the white hare leaping, see the white hare!

At the Great Gate

Now I shall take my boat again
and row out through the grey rain
to the cold salt blaze of the sun

I shall rock out there in the loneliness
the silence that is no man's business
till the winds open and let me pass

to the sudden crying of a hundred gulls.

The Book at Lismore*

Ten roaring ballads
relating to the life of Finn

fifty lochside lyrics
in very tricky measures

and a handful
of rank indecencies.

For MacDiarmid*

Scotland in winter
wind whooming round the white peaks

I have been walking along the river Druie
by the golden pine and the silver birch
thinking of your poetry

now in the Lairig Ghru
at the heart of the ontological landscape
alone with the diamond body.

McTaggart*

What was he after there at Machrihanish
this man whose painting
the little critics said had no finish?

(that sense of windswept space
sea and sky in multiple movement
landscape seen as mindscape
the human figures
more and more transparent
till they disappeared)

if the question had been put to him directly
he would have made no answer
simply walked a little farther along the shore.

Pool Poem for MacCaig*

1. *The classical pool*
Not the golden, but the silver age
the clear, cool light of a distant sun
get that coolness on to the page
and your latin homework will be done.

2. *The gaelic pool*
I'm a celtic text not yet gathered in
Duncan Ban knew me, and Rob Donn too
my gaelic tongue ripples round every stone
between Lochinver and Kylesku.

3. *The philosophical pool*
Plato was naïve compared to me
that ideal system was one big bore
I'm about as deep as a pool can be
unsystematic, but ideas galore.

Dunbar*

A Saturday night late October
in John Muir's town
night falling and the rain
over the old red stone

offshore, fifty sea-crows
standing dusky on a rock
while the Bass light fitfully blinks
far out in the windy dark.

Happy at Hyères

In memoriam R. L. Stevenson

'I was happy only once –
that was at Hyères'

often his eyes were sore
and at times he coughed blood

yet life, after all, was good

sure, it was a pity
to have to churn out tushery
(that *Black Arrow* thing or, worse, *Prince Otto*)
just to make a little money

but there were golden islands
out there on the horizon

and around the house a garden
where he could walk at ease
breathing in the scent of blue-gummed trees.

François Villon

Mes jours s'en sont allés errant

Half-dead at thirty-two
banned from Paris, he made for Poitou

hardly regretting *auld lang syne*:
bad women and worse wine

another life, hell, what a hope
existentially, Frank was no dope

he'd hole up somewhere in some small town
and wait till death came to mow him down

be ye man, he thought, or pig or bird
'damn it all ' is the final word

but the sun shone and the wind blew
along that high road down to Poitou.

Three American Beers[*]

> Damariscotta, State of Maine,
> that Autumn.

1. Moosehead

About Moosehead
there isn't that much to be said

'quality ... tradition
oldest ... independent'

OK, great

just remember
'drinking it will impair
your ability to drive a car'

I won't be driving any cars, man
I'm doing this route strictly on foot

what gets to me
is the quizzical look
in that moose's eye.

2. Katahdin Red

This is where
you begin to hear the wolves howling

'the Indian word
for great mountain'

hops from the Pacific Northwest
pure water
native American yeast

I'm drinking this one
in memory of Henry

'Talk of mysteries! Think of our life in nature:
rocks, trees, wind on our faces –
the solid earth, the common sense!
Who are we, where are we?'

3. Mack Arctic

This one I see
looking more closely
got imported from Norway

'First on the North Pole '

clean arctic water
from snowcovered mountains

I go back out
into the moony, windy street
with an enormous metafuzzical
question on my mind

was that there bear
going into hibernation
or coming out of it?

Pushkin 1837

The white nights of St Petersburg

reading Kracheninnikov's
Description of Kamchatka

those rivers:
the Avatcha
the Amschigatch
the Schiaktaou
the Ouikoal

those names

that langage, that space
(with such powerful reality
no need to be 'poetical')

what a hellish pity
to have to leave it all
for a duel with a fool.

Mandelstam

While the symbolists and the acmeists
the futurists, the imagists and the constructivists
were at fisticuffs in Moscow

he liked to go away on his own
and wander round the shores of the Black Sea

'listening at the limits of the world
to the silence of beginnings'

what, in his eyes
the Revolution had done
was to pulverize
identity and person

'it's whitened
at the foaming crest of the wave
that we acquire a new tongue'

what mattered finally
was a line of rough stone
left by a chaos of unidentified forces
and a few fundamental forms
called from all kinds of languages.

The Study at Culross*

The lower room is full of objects
history's ordered bric-a-brac
in which visitors inherently bored
show intelligent interest

The upper room is still empty
there (in that small cartesian cell)
remains the merest chance
for the essential to happen.

At Laon

Vox volatilis

The Romans called it Laudunum
turning it into a garrison
before them
it was a little old Gaulish town
devoted to the god of light

it was in this place Charles the Bald
gathered together all the Scotic scholars
who, having crossed the rough seas,
were scattering over the continent

among them John Erigena
who worked there in the *scriptorium*
at translations from the Greek
with an occasional poem

'There is no language for being
you can only outline it
with poetic intelligence'

there was a 'Scots quarter' in this town
and over the centuries
a street called the Rue des Écossais
till some municipal clown
turned it into the Street of Echoes.

Report to Erigena*

Sunt lumina

'Labour' suddenly seems exactly right
hard slogging, no facility
like learning the basis of a grammar
working your way into unknown logic

it's earth in labour makes for diamond

here on this nameless shore, knowing the work
who are the workers? who the travellers?
reality works – wonders? travel-travail

the old signs come out of the morning
the skull fills and empties with the tide
energy gathered, the first act

ragged coast, rugged, rough winds
the language bears us, bares us

rock province, roots – and lights.

Arthur Schopenhauer in Frankfurt

A vulgo longe longeque remotus

At Fair View, number sixteen
a statue of Buddha and a bust of Kant
discouraged any facile talk

whatever can be better, he thought
than the meditative gathering of the mind
in some idiosyncratic retreat?

all his life he'd laboured at a work
unknown not only to public at large
but to the myopic crew of philosophical folk

no matter, it would remain

the October sun had come out
in a spread of luminous white
from a morning of rain

'Atman', he said to his dog, 'let's go for a walk'.

Reading Marpa in the Blue Mountains*

When the tiger year was ending
weary of the business of the world
I came away into the wilderness

the elements of wind and water seethed
the dark hills were clad in white

I don't philosophize but I keep at my task
I sleep little and meditate often

when named at all I am the man apart.

Tones

'Play this verse
in the *tsing tse* key'
said Confucius to his pupils
'which is the key of melancholy'

'Let them', thought Chuang Tzu
as he walked in the hills alone
'but there's a stiller, darker key than that
it's called the Ground Tone'.

Stations on the Way

1. Shirakawa

Here the northern regions begin:

trees thick with red foliage
sound of the autumn wind

white grasses at the roadside.

(for Bashô)

2. Shôno

All day the heavy rain falling

holding my pack on my back
feet slipping in the mud

station 46 on the Tokaido Road.

(for Hiroshige)

Temple near Snowy Mountains

It must be hellish cold:
the water's still moving round the rocks
but the trees are frozen stiff

white roofs of the temple
there in the rough dark wood

and a little fellow with a big hat
walking head down along the shore

Fan K'wan painted it on silk
round about the millennium.

Sesshu*

After years in China

emptiness achieved

he painted

with the fewest of strokes

the hardness of rocks

the twistedness of roots.

Kenkô*

When he died, 8th April, 1350
fragments of writing were found
in the hermitage at Yoshida

a few poems pasted on the walls

Shôtetsu brought them together
under the title: *Tsurezure-gusa*
'Jottings made in idle hours'

Shinto, Tao, Buddha, K'ong
were all present in this monk's mind:
'O, characters traced by my brush
guide me at length to the pure land.'

Round North Again*

>Going back home

1.
A blue-grey stillness
where the dark waters flow –
night of the heron.

2.
That branch among the fern
was a red stag
sheltering from the rain.

3.
Why did he return
to that empty island?
bog-cotton in the wind.

4.
Storm brewing
the world about to fall apart –
the cormorant's black cackle.

5.
A grey shore
and a battered herring-box:
Scott of Stornoway.

A Short Lesson in Gaelic Grammar*

The small stone is white
(*tha a' clach bheag ban*)
the white stone is small
(*tha a' clach bhan beag*)
the stone is small and white
(*tha a' clach beag, ban*)

the small stones are white
(*tha na clachan beaga ban*)
the white stones are small
(*tha na clachan bana beag*)
the stones are small and white
(*tha na clachan beag, ban*).

Carmen Gadelicum

On Celtic honey and other mindblowing substances

This late, very late September
with the sun getting smaller and smaller
the bees are busy hour after hour

buzzing like McKenzies

another agitated character
is Calum's nephew Hector
holed up in a cave on far Mhic Fearchair

sniffing glue and chewing benzies.

Late Autumn on the Findhorn River

Making her way
through October mist
amid rough grey granite
and gleaming schist

red rowan, silver birch
lining her banks

up in that high North-East corner

sleek animals
bound alongside her
alone or in bands

till she reaches her mouth
at the Moray Firth
with Arctic gulls yelling
over barren sands.

At St Matthew's Point

In Brittany, that Spring

When Matthew fared out from Galilee
he was making vaguely for the Celtic Sea

over there, at the end of the land
he met old Enoch, with a book in his hand

since he himself had written a book
Matthew was eager to have a look

'it's all about wind and rock and wave
how they're born and how they behave'

'what about God and love and sin
what salvation is there in a fish's fin?'

old Enoch, he made no reply
just kept gazing at sea and sky

Matthew thought, this is something new
I'll stick around for a year or two.

Black Forest

>Heidegger at home

On the steep slope
of a mountain valley
a little chalet
eighteen feet by twenty

all around
meadow and pinewood

when snow surrounded the house
that was the time for philosophy:
following all those
secret, silent paths
till cogitation turned into sight

like this high summer morning
and two hawks gliding
round and round
in the absolute light.

Northern Trail

1.
Dark waters, home
of greylag goose, blackthroated
diver
salmon, charr and trout ...
after ten days' drought
the rain has returned
a grey smir
obscuring the loch, smooring
the hills.

2.
Chill dawn air
this rock:
those Ice Age scratchings
and there a hillock
a fox's lookout
(the grass has greened
with his droppings).

3.
Birch grove
silver-blurred in the rain
the bleached trunk
of a dead
pine
deer-print
in the peaty ground.

4.
Burn water grey
club moss
tight on the stones
and a single
arctic
black-stamened
white-petalled
flower.

5.
Down there
along the rock and scree
a ptarmigan
makes it over the ridge.

Autobiography

Each star
in its own sudden fire
blazes
or shoots
in a fast fine curve of light
over the breathing emptiness
and leaves me
alone by the rock
or stumbling
groping my way
through the undergrowth
with only
the feeling of existence
as it trembles in an animal's belly.

The Most Difficult Area

To attain the most difficult area

pine branches golden grotesquely shaped
thrusting out from the parent stem

to attain the most difficult area

pebble smooth-led by the tide over gravel
now held in a seeing hand, complete

to attain the most difficult area

bird skeleton found this day on the moor
flight and flesh in the ultimate nakedness

to attain the most difficult area.

Beinn Airidh Charr[*]

There is a colder, clearer substance
on the other side of this ignorance

it is these hills, blazing
with a sanity that leaves thought behind
this light that is
the limit of austerity
and makes words blind

only in the brain, erratically
an icy ecstasy.

A High Blue Day on Scalpay*

This is the summit of contemplation, and
    no art can touch it
blue, so blue, the far-out archipelago
    and the sea shimmering, shimmering
no art can touch it, the mind can only
    try to become attuned to it
to become quiet, and space itself out, to
    become open and still, unworlded
knowing itself in the diamond country, in
    the ultimate unlettered light.

My Properties

I'm a landowner myself after all –
I've got twelve acres of white silence
up at the back of my skull.

On Rannoch Moor*

1.
Here, where the glacier started
snow hardening into ice and
slowly moving –
sculpting the tertiary terrain.

2.
This morning
(a few millennia later)
a chill wind blowing
on original ground.

3.
An erratic boulder
let it be the centre
from it, the eye travels
tracing the circle ...

4.
In the midst
of this beautiful desolation
no voices
only whispered whisperings.

5.
The other animals
make their presence felt
grouse whirring up from the heather
two crows scudding for the gully.

6.
Was that a deer
or a snag of withered wood
(over there, a hare
ears raised attentively).

7.
Walking round the lochan:
those gold-coloured gramina
fixed in blue ice –
radical phenomena.

8.
Looking round again
from rock to dark rock
and up along
the white horizon…

9.
On this plateau
has taken place
the ultimate union
of matter and space.

Road Fragment

My thanks for this handful of April days
for the white wind blowing
for the dark earth and the tangled grass
and the woman beside me walking

        (Twelve Ben Country, Ireland)

Early Morning Light on Loch Sunart*

While I write this
a grey heron
is standing motionless
in the early morning light
of Loch Sunart

At the centre
of a ring of silence
a grey heron
only the waters rippling
(language dare not be loud this morning)

For still words (long fallen silent)
listen (if you will) to these:
gheibte bradan fioruisg ann
a' direadh ris gach sruth
eoin an t' -sleibh gu lionmhor

A grey heron
watching, listening
in an early morning
glitter of waters –
maybe dreaming?

Fishing in nothingness
(that is one way of putting it)
here on Loch Sunart
bright falling of the year
quiet, so quiet.

Near Point of Stoer

Full moon
and a wind from the North

little sleep tonight

up at four
walking along
a silent shore

trying to translate
into a tongue that's known
a poem writ
in the language of stone.

Alba*

So much has gone
now there is only the sun

the sun up there
white-golden, bare

maybe not free
but full of its own necessity

it's a world-morning
and I sit here rock-like breathing

breathing toward the sun.

Letter to an Old Calligrapher

A hundred days
along shore and mountain

with eye open
for heron and cormorant

now writing this
at the world's edge

in a silence become
a second nature

coming to know
in brain and in bone

the path of emptiness.

Rannoch Moor Once More

Sheep trintles
a wisp of wool
buzzing fly.

Obscure

Golden eagle
red deer
would be
almost too much

I'll settle for
this arctic moss
on the rock's
obscure face.

Into the Whiteness

Now I have burnt all my knowledge
and am learning to live with the whiteness naked

what I call art now is nothing made
but the pure pathology of my body and mind

at the heart of a terrible and joyous world.

Winter Letter from the Mountain*

In this world
always harder and more acrid
more and more white

you ask me for news?

the ice breaks in blue characters
who can read them?

I talk grotesquely to myself
and the silence answers.

Mountain and Glacier World*

Arrived at this point
where the whiteness is manifest
here in the mountains
where the coldness my element
surrounds me with eternity

arrived at this point
the high crest of nothingness
where the 'I' has no meaning
and the self is ecstatically
alone with its aloneness

shall I blow out my brains?

Late December by the Sound of Jura*

Red bracken on the hills
rain snow hail and rain
the deer are coming down
the lochs gripped in ice
the stars blue and bright

I have tried to write to friends
but there is no continuing
I gaze out over the Sound
and see hills gleaming in the icy sun.

Rosy Quartz

Out of what storm of darkness
out of what hellish blaze
out of what torments and what changes

held at last in a crystal matrix
held at last in its own wild form
held in its own unbroken aura

came this incandescent stone
came this immaculate glory
came this idea of the earth

to illuminate the frozen sky.

Fossil

In chalky stone

some day
God knows how many
million years ago

the claw of a bird
and *raindrops*.

Theory*

1.
The white cell almost in darkness
outside: rocks in abruption, sea-
silence wavering. It is there.

2.
Rough shape, clifted, that kwartz
chaos-given, ashored, tide-washed and
in the good space gazed-at.

3.
Cast – the first stone; only the
thrust and the not-silver, not-white, not-crystal
splash – no reading in the widening circles.

4.
Great reason grasped, the twelve-worded orator
walks on the shingle
with quiet eyes.

Example

As a thin blaze of quartz in sandstone
has behind it the whole of geology
and in its purity is beyond perfection.

Blue Thistle Sermon

Blue thistle on the dunes
blue burning thistle on the dunes
its roots in sand
but sturdy as hell

the sun beats
on me and the blue thistle
this long afternoon

I contemplate the blue thistle
and the blue thistle contemplates damn all.

Late Summer Journey*

The afternoon
washed itself out with rain
and a little rainbow
appeared above Barra
almost too good to be true

two hours later
all the blues having changed into greys
South Uist was a chain of black islands
lit coldly by the moon.

Ludaig Jetty

The small motorboat has puttered its way
out to the fishing
the bus has passed by
to collect the children for school
the red postal van
has delivered the mail

now here at Ludaig jetty
there is only
the wind and the light
the cry of a peewit
and the lip-lip-lipping
of grey water on white sand.

Beatus

Eighth century

At a lonely monastery
high in the hills of septentrion Spain
his principal study
the Book of Revelation
commentary after commentary

'the prophets had made the field ready
the apostles did the reaping'

a long and arduous way it was
from the apple-girl to the Apocalypse...

to get the story clear in his head
to see how the world was set out now
he would paint a chart

up in the east, the initial garden
the Mediterranean, open to the west
to the north, obscurities: Pannonia, Albania

over there in the south
beyond the broad crimson belt
of the Erythrean Sea
territory totally unknown
'desert ground, scorched by the sun'

hard to make up one's mind
about what it all added up to
and where it would end...

but the artwork was satisfactory

as he put in the final finishing touches
a frieze of islands and slim blue fishes
sunrise was burning the Asturias.

Carta Rarissima

After so many cogitations and calculations
at last I have it

that 18th century
French map of Scotland

the country lying on its side
in a darkblue solitude

giving rise by erosion
to a hundred islands

what is this Scotland?
a continent and an archipelago
a unity and a scattering

with the map laid out
on a floor in the old town of Edinburgh
I gaze on it
gloating

intellectually gallivanting.

Letter from Cape Wrath

Interfluvial archipelagoes

excentric
excessive
exposed

high cliffs
deep clefts

topography
suddenly interrupted
brutally sundered

ravines
fissures
gaps

gullies
creeks
grottoes

lines of force
lines of fragility

powers of erosion
hierarchies of resistance

masses of drift
cloaks of moraine
abrased platforms

lithology

littorality.

Last Page of a Notebook*

'*Fuzeshin, fuzebutsu, fuzemotsu*'

A bird yell
emptied my skull

ricks of hay
lined the fields

a fishing smack
lay at quiet anchor –

it was Kyle of Tongue
on a blue morning.

BOOK III

Walking the Coast

The need for panorama and perspective. This long poem of fifty-three waves is a recapitulation of my living up to that date, a summing-up (*summa scotica poetica*) of the whole Scottish mindscape, and a map of new co-ordinates. Tidal analogies, Atlantic poetics.

I

....
                for the question is always
how
           out of all the chances and changes
      to select
     the features of real significance
              so as to make
    of the welter
      a world that will last
and how to order
            the signs and the symbols
   so they will continue
    to form new patterns
   developing into
new harmonic wholes
    so to keep life alive
in complexity
    and complicity
             with all of being –
there is only poetry.

II*

   living as a boy on the shore
 seeing and hearing
    the clou –
  ding and clamouring of gulls
 like overwhelming metaphors
    or maybe a heron
'na h'aonar ri taobh na tuinne
mar thuigse leatha fhèin 's a' chruinne
  alone beside the sea
 like a mind alone in the universe.

III*

ah, the gulls:
    baagies   bluemaws   aulins   badochs
  goos   scutiallans
          cobbies and *scarts*
colmows   collochans fraiks
      and   *scawreys*
    dungbirds   diviegoos   goylers   merricks
            pictarns   pickseas
     dirtyallans
pleengies   redshanks   scoultons
                  swabies
   tarrocks and *weathergaws* –
  all haphazardly manoeuvring
      a hymn to chaoticism
        out in the wind
  and the lifting waters
and myself there maybe no more
      staring from my mind's wide-open door
   than *faoileag an droch chladaich*
  the gull of a stony shore.

IV*

    in that house of three storeys
        only yards from the sea
   a house with
       anwar don lavar
       levawr wrthi
   a wild wave talking
        and clashing beside it.

V

    and outside in the darkness
           the island lighthouse
      a white tower
          36 feet high
with the focal plane 90 feet
          above high water
     showing a white group-flashing light
with the characteristic
     of 2 flashes in quick succession
every 30 seconds
  its effective intensity
being 200.000 candlepower
     its range in clear weather
    16 miles.

VI

    and how it began was
  there in the womb of the hills
      seeing that snowhill
            smooring against the sky
        rooted there
           obscure
amazed
           inarticulate
                    strange
  then a cry.

VII

goddess
    dark wind blowing in from the sea
        this dawn
  the deep-blue mussel-beds
          writhe and crackle
      the salt sand
        reflects in its pools
            the awakened gulls
  and the first
        redness
     as you open your belly
        over the island
  and the day comes cold and howling.

VIII

like the still warm ashes
    of a fire of wood
        is the heron's body
  now silent at the edge
      of its uncouth nest
in the beech's crest
motionless in its swaying heights
    and myself there watching
among the red leaves
    that litter the earth
winter's torn branches
and
  signs of birth
those blue shells
    clotted with blood
  that smell of the sea.

IX

Canadian firs
    their branches lopped
        eyes carved in the bark
eyes
a circle white-yellow
    surrounding the dark red
        centre wood
resin dripping clear and brown
    from the eye-wound
and the sap
    turning in the air
        to a milky blue –

who in the stillness
    gazes here?

X

a scurry of red leaves
    and the wind passes over
rippling the stream
    the wind is all around
but only stray gusts enter
    the wood's dark centre
enter and are gone –
    only scurrying leaves
        and the rippled stream.

XI

                              believing
              that the biological
                              aim of art
                is to project around us
        the images
                the proofs
                        the manifestations
                of a power of synthesis
                        at one with life
                and maintaining life
against solitude
                and fragmentation
                the cold aggressiveness
                        of the space-time world.

XII

                      and
that the surface of things
            can give enjoyment or disgust
      but the inwardness of things
                gives life
knowing that the poetry
           which says that inwardness
                also gives life.

XIII

    like
at the turn of the path
  in the April wood:
 that small world
       complex
              fortuitous
    drenched with brightness
earth
   stones
       wet grass
and the red
   branches of the hawthorn –
outside only the moors
and the bleakness of the glacial drift.

XIV

    or like the group of alpine flowers
            on the heights of Ben Lawers:
              saxifrage
        mountain pansy
  gentian
                wood-anemone
     rose-root
                 moss-campion
       angelica
            dwarf marigold
– a unique assemblage
        due to a series of coincidences
a small stratum of ideal rock
        well-mineral'd
    not over-acid as in surrounding strata
        on mountains so high
            that unstable habitats
have existed there continuously
        since the post-glacial period
  the plants becoming
        established in a crack
their roots breaking up the rock
        by a slow process
their shoots and leaves
        collecting rock fragments
    blown by the wind
or washed down by water
        till the soil becomes deeper
and the flowers
    can gather full nourishment
        and beauty grow.

XV

the loveliness is everywhere
        even
    in the ugliest
        and most hostile environment
the loveliness is everywhere
    at the turning of a corner
            in the eyes
    and on the lips
        of a stranger
    in the emptiest areas
        with no place for hope
    and only death
        to invite the heart
the loveliness is there
    it emerges
    incomprehensible
        inexplicable
    it rises in its own reality
and what we must learn is
        how to receive it
    into ours.

XVI

 the pebble of rough
    and unprepossessing stone
   the harsh dull case
     splits open
 to reveal
    the lovely agate crystal
   the boulder
      cut asunder
   shows
  a blue-gleaming layer of amethyst –
  there is a principle
 of beauty and order
    at the heart of chaos
   within life there is life.

XVII

it will come again
        the living thought
    certain as those wings
           that catch the light
and exact in its loveliness
    certain as those wings
       and
    exact in its loveliness
         the living thought
it will come again.

XVIII*

in the period of spiritual drought
    said Kokoschka
the essential values will survive
    in spite of all
and then will come the future...
    I am no defeatist
        neither optimist nor pessimist
    what I know
is what I see
    like a stone falling
    like stars gleaming...
and why do I squander my life-time painting
    because when I am painting
I know myself in the midst
    of something living.

XIX

for out of the darkness
                        suddenly
                    came the white-haired gulls
                    came starlings
                          grotesquely
and thrushes blackies redbreasts
                    noisily
    end of winter movements
        colours movements
                    in my space
daffodil
      crocus
                primrose
a girl's face
      now what I know
               must grow
        rain
            earth.

XX*

    living in obscurity
        like Hakuyu
      his name meant
          White Obscurity
      his name meant
          he who lived in the hills
        back of Northern White Water –
or secretly though not unconsciously
      in the cities of Europe
    living my life
        founding and grounding
   a world.

XXI

                for the higher mind
       is like unto a lump of rosy quartz
            a curious rock
whose deep and unified rose-shade
                 is rare in the extreme
      but which even when pale
                    (as when over-heated
       or exposed to strong sunlight
              it loses its colour)
can be restored absolutely
            to its original state
    by complete secretion away for a while
  in a place of darkness
            wet
               and cold.

XXII

the rosy quartz –
    there in loose pieces
on the beach of Coll
    in granite belts
on the north shore of Loch Eatharna
    and in gneiss
at Poolewe Glen Logan and Rona:
an image of the soul
    when it emerges at last
from the *magma originaria*
      and through the conflicts –
an idea of the earth.

XXIII

      having lived in Germany
            domiciled in Munich
        (soft snow drifting over Schwabing)
in a shack
    where I nearly froze to death
        on the edge of the *Englischer Garten*
          (thin grassblades held in frost)
  listening at night
     to the blind man's radio
           howling
   knowing every painting in the *Haus der Kunst*
      having climbed
          with my cold barbarian eyes
     every baroque pillar in the city
       finding no paradise.

XXIV*

   and Munch
      asked about the book he was writing
    the autobiography
        answered
  'I
      have put it aside
    it is
  nothing but chaos
        nothing
            but
                chaos'
 and
  'I am very lonely here' he said
    'but I go on
        working quietly'.

XXV*

it was of Goethe
        that Groddeck wrote:
  'He understood
   the great secret
  and tried
     to live his life
        in accordance with it
         merging his separate existence
      in the life of nature
and this is the reason
       why we feel him
    so strange and yet familiar
     so cold and remote
   yet brimming over with energy
         and life-determination'.

XXVI

in Paris also
>where
from my little window
>on the 7th floor
I could see the red light
>on the Eiffel Tower
pointing the obscurity
>I breathed in.

XXVII*

    having lived in Glasgow
           lodged in a large dark room
      with three shelves of books
          a table a chair a bed
        on the floor a rough carpet
  (Connemara red)
          in one corner a rug
  (a goatskin from Tibet)
on the first wall was pinned
        a print of Hokusai
on the second was
           an X-ray photo of my ribs
on the third was
      a long quotation from Nietzsche
on the fourth was
          nothing at all
  that's the wall I went through
    before I arrived here.

XXVIII

        knowing now
        that the life
    at which I aim
             is a circumference
continually expanding
    through sympathy and
           understanding
rather than an exclusive centre
    of pure self-feeling
    the whole I'm out for
        is centre plus circumference
and now the struggle at the centre is over
        the circumference
             beckons from everywhere.

XXIX*

                    for
            like Kandinsky
returning to his studio at twilight
    and seeing a canvas
        'of indescribable
            and incandescent beauty'
it happens
    that the 'known' materials of my life
sunk almost into oblivion
            by familiarity
    suddenly blaze out
            materia poetica
of new realities
        each time more complex
        and I advance.

XXX*

   so that when a physicist
                far out in his field
      says the starting-point
        for the realm of unknowns
          is a
    'universe of contrasts
           grouped into
       complexes of relations
    with aspects of
        order and disorder
     including
        change and tendency'
I say that's it
    that's my territory
    that's the world I'm living through
         and trying to work out.

XXXI*

    and when a Japanese literatus
        speaks of the series of *waka* poems
    (sometimes as many as a hundred in a sequence)
           written in the Kamakura period
                (13th and 14th centuries)
        saying 'the result
            was often a kind of kaleidoscopic beauty
                with infinite variety
        revealed to the reader
            in a slowly evolving movement'
I recognize my aim.

XXXII

    even crystals
           know disorder and shadow
        but since our aim is not perfection
             but natural form
                    in movement
      this will not deter us
        or cause us
    to plunge ourselves into
        morbid disintegration
    we must think in reality clearly
      knowing that
given a sufficiently
    complex ground of signs
        even the most acute
of the problems of disorder
          may be solved
      through what is called
          semi-classical approximation.

XXXIII*

'Who, if I cried
        would hear me
    from the ranks of angels
   and even if suddenly one
       should take me to his heart
I would perish of his stronger presence
   for the Beautiful is nothing
        but the onset of the Terrible
   still just endurable
   and we admire it so
        that serenely
    disdains to destroy us
        every angel is terrible
so I hold myself in check and swallow
      the darkly-sobbing call
   alas whom then can we use
     not angels not men
and the cunning animals
     have noticed already
   that we are none too securely
     at home
   in the interpreted world'.

XXXIV

                let us speak no more of angels
but of the Great Skua
      skimming down
           the east coast of Scotland
                with startling cries
           in a windy and white september
or of the Grey Heron
           flustering to rest
    with outstretched shanks
            and a fraiking throat
after lonely fishing
        on the Ayrshire coast
        on a darkblue august evening.

XXXV

for the moment now
>   is as the one marked so
> on the barometer
>   > set in the wall
>   at North Street
>   > in the town of St Andrews
> (a redness on the water
>   > this April morning
>   low grund and sharring of the waves
>   > against the pier) –
> 'when rise begins
>   > after low squalls
>   expect clear blow'.

XXXVI*

    now here in the north
           beyond the barren red
       in the ootbrecks
        ortan in this husky weather
           at my owdny of a poem
     living out on this grand
          that runs into the sea
      with fanns of whiteness
        drifting up against my windows
writing in goliment
      till I get da whole fargis
    on to da page
          tinks du I'll make it
      by God I will try.

XXXVII

in this house
>   where the wood on the stone
>   burns brightly red
> this house
>   where the candle
> glows with a lithe
>   blue-hearted flame
>   this house
> where the girl's gull-body
>   lies in her nakedness
> and the high north wind
> has been blowing now
>   for ten white days.

XXXVIII*

   there's only one man here
         to keep me company
     and that's Thomas of Cromarty
          his ghost
     who is a walking gramary
   and *Altus Prosator* in person
         craggy and crazy
     like a crop of lewisian gneiss
        overlooking the coast
   with seven types... of lightning
          flickering round its crest
     and
deep in the heart of its darkness
      belly-laughing chaos.

XXXIX

Urquhart
    inherits a 'crazed estate'
        in the extreme north of Scotland
sets himself up a library
    (later confiscated by usurers)
    with books gathered from sixteen countries
        in the mansion of Cromarty
    and writes
        a pedantic and fantastic
            treatise on trigonometry
        called *Trissotetras*
    a *Pantoxponoxanon*
            to deduce the genealogy
of the Urquharts
    from the red earth in the hands of God
    a translation of Rabelais'
        Gargantua and *Pantagruel*
  and *Logopandecteision*
    an introduction
to the possibilities
    of framing 'a new idiome
    of far greater perfection'
than all existent languages
for all
  'pregnant and ingenious spirits'
      dying
    at the age of about sixty
    suddenly
on the continent
    in a fit of excessive laughter.

XL*

   though I think too at times
       of Donnacha ban nan Orain
  whose wife
         was a dandy whisky distiller –
and of Alasdair MacMhaigstir Alasdair
     the man who wrote the *birlinn* –
        and of Iain MacCodrum nan Ron
     who wrote the rabelaisian
         Oran na Muice
     and who chose an enormous and amorphous
  lump of gneiss
       for his gravestone –
and of Hugh MacDiarmid
      composing the caledonian wake
     circumveiloped in obscuritads
      and
ortan like an ox in an ootdyke.

XLI*

    and *larus atricilla*
                      Laughing Gull
            pagophila eburnea
            Ivory Gull
      rhodostethia rosea
                    Rosy Gull
      these also
                  are here in the darkness
        totems gleaming in the night
                  like *adee*
      the Kwakiutl thunderbird
      up there
in the High Northwest of America
    for this is my potlatch poem
(since
    as father Rabelais says
      '*heureux nous resputons*
              si à autruy
tousjours donnons
            et eslargissons beaucoup')
      being one of those
      '*beaulx livres*
           de haulte graisse'
      that must come out of this time
           for survival
  so Indians Chinese and Eskimos
           scientists and fellow-poets
    all souls of our delirious earth
        grant me help
      come succour my brain
        I am saying my prayers
for the first time in years
        I need everything.

XLII

   having no matter where I be
                  a studio in the wood
   as in this Chinese painting now before me
      ground of tree rock earth grass
      cut by precipitous waters
             painted by the monk Shang-jui
1729
        in the style of T'ang Yin
           one of the Four Great Masters.

XLIII

        living and writing at random
    but knowing
      that
though living at random
          there is a tendency to stress
  the essential in the random.

XLIV*

    following the path
that 'path compendious
  deviating from common obliquity'
    which Michael Scot
  the leading mind in western Europe
in the early 13th century
    an *'internationalgebildeter Mann'*
with a mass of knowledge
    crystallising in his brain
  into shining thought
and a love of complexity
      that makes him delight
in distinguishing say
  sidus from *astrum* and
    both from *stella*
and all three from
  signum imago or *planeta*
(repugnant to content himself
  with a numb generic)
calls
    'the way of true science
which is poetry's commencement'.

XLV

the poem being
            what happens when
  a welter of substantial
            feelings and facts
have passed through the thalamus
            the belly of the brain
  and ascended
            without shortcircuiting
right up into the cortical region
    from where
            abstracted
  they return again
            worded on the tongue.

XLVI

elsewise
>> an attempt
> to get at and say out
all
that the world comprises
> which man
only rarely
> realises.

XLVII

  or again
        like the lightning that leaps
     from the percussion of stones
       like the
    thin blue ripple of light
      made by the swing of an axe in the air
     like the easy
climb and curve of a wave
        and its free fall into foam.

XLVIII*

  and finally
     a complex symbol
  placing the accent
      on the union of contraries
  stressing
     the one in the many
the possible
     difficult harmony
 in the human conscience
   the ἁρμονία of Heraclitus.

XLIX

   but always
                exemplary language
        subtle as flowers
                plastic as waves
flexible as twigs
                    powerful as wind
       concentred as rock
   syncratic
            as the self
       beautiful as love.

L

   some like the girasol
       turn their blossom to the sun
     some bloom only in the dark
        like the cereus
        that waits on midnight
or the convolvulus
        that unfolds
   its moonlike petals
       with the setting sun
     perhaps the simplicity
of the wood anemone
         its serenity
       its direct access
  to the energy of the sun
        and the richness of the earth
    might have evolved
         a quieter fuller brain
than the hurry-scurry of zoological existence
      on which we have depended.

LI

who has not observed it
        the primal movement
    the play of wind on water
            the undulation
      the glassy membrane
lifted
    excited
          and energised
    by insisting air
       the curving
           the deliberate inflection
   the flurry of whiteness
         the bright cast of spray
the long falling rush
       and the hundredfold ripple.

LII

even if we had only
> those few scattered rocks on the shore
>> (the wind tonight
> blowing hard with rain over the sea)
>> how much
> there would be to be learned
>> for it is possible
> to live with the rocks
>> in unity of mind

and perhaps one who knows
>> even one rock thoroughly
> in all its idiosyncracy
>> and relatedness
> to sea and sky
is better fit to speak
>> to another human being

than one who lives and rots perpetually
> in a crowded society
> that teaches him
>> nothing essential.

LIII

like this rock now before me
    facing the tide
  an outcrop
    of dark grey sandstone
      (so the ones on which
        as children
we chiselled our signs)
  with a blaze
    of white granite
running right through it –

    understand this, poet.

BOOK IV

The Bird Path

Moving between North and South, West and East. The bird path (a way for the opening of being and the development of mind) goes back ultimately to shamanism, and was much elaborated in extreme buddhism. It goes round the world. I travel it on my own wings, in my own ways.

At the Sign of the Rosy Gull*

'When we awoke we journeyed towards the north, strangers'
(George Seferis: *Mythistorema*)

1.
The ivory gull is beautiful, and one of the toughest birds in the world. Doesn't live in an ivory tower. Unless you call the hell-gates of the Arctic an ivory tower.

Then there's the laughing gull. O, how she laughs. She's a crazy sea-screamer. Nests in the skull of a ghost.

But the rosy gull – there's more about her than a man can say. She has a white head and breast, rose-flushed, and is one of the mystic birds of the world. Few, very few ornithologists have seen her alive.

I love all gulls, but the rosy gull is the one that forever possesses me. I see her suddenly now and then, when I speak out largely and clear. I'd like others to see her too. Some people just won't believe that she exists.

They prefer canaries in cages. Or parrots. Or pterodactyls with the whooping cough. I suppose I'm just illiterate.

2.
It was on that shore in the west I first saw the Rosy Gull, about fifteen years ago. My sister had told me there was a horse's head just above the waterline to the north of the pier, and I had gone down to see and hide it away among the rocks under the pier till the flesh should rot off and I be able to retrieve the skull.

I had found the head and was dragging it along the sand when I discovered also this carcass of a seagull. It was unlike any seagull I had ever seen. Its breast feathers were lightly rose-coloured and I thought at first it was blood, but the bird was not wounded, and blood anyway could not cause such beautiful coloration. That was the Rosy Gull, and how it ever came to arrive there on that shore is just one more mystery added to the great mystery of its life.

For having seen such a strange gull that day, I could not rest till I had at least identified her, and found out something of her habits and habitat. This I did by looking up all the bird-books I could lay my hands on.

The results of my investigations were these: this Rosy Gull or Ross's Gull is usually considered the most beautiful of all birds in the world. Very little is known about her. In the arctic winter, when all other birds go south, the Rosy Gull heads north and winters probably in the very central parts of the Polar Sea, where harsh gales prevail and almost complete darkness...

Poem to My Coat

> 'My coat's all worn after so many years
> Shreds of it are blowing in the wind'
> (Bokuju)

1.
Rain, earth and salt
have worked themselves into the cloth

the perfume of girls
the stench of cities

old coat
with the familiar stink of life

let us go on another journey.

2.
Let us penetrate once again
the pelagian country

the body of our early love

happy to walk the rocks
and to move among gulls

through an easy ecstasy

heading northwards
in the arctic light.

3.
And the wind comes to meet us
the cold wind of dawn

with a book in one hand
a lump of quartz in the other

and a gull on his shoulder

greeting us like a brother
who's been away in foreign parts

more difficult areas

welcoming us in gaelic
(the three phrases he remembers)

and refreshing us
with a little rain distilled

by his sister the west.

4.
Walking along the shore
remembering the past

grasping it in several ways
the better to know it

and penetrate beyond appearances
into the secret nerve:

pelagian orgies
pushed to the limit!

5.
Old shamanskin, listen
while we're moving farther on

this poem is for you
I'll pin it on your lining

may we remain long together
through all kinds of weather

and enjoy the travelling.

The Shaman's Way

1.
I was called out
the big sky spoke to me
the dark wood spoke to me
the fire spoke to me
I was called out

I didn't want to go
a girl was giving me smiles
I didn't want to go
but I was called out

I fasted nine days
and then nine days
then nine days more

I saw the moon wax and wane
I saw the path of the wind
I saw a river in the sky
I saw a flight of blue stars
I saw a sea
that was milky and misty
and islands full of birds

sleeping in a tree's roots
I had dreams and dreams:
strange language, strange
like the trembling of a thousand leaves

noises and nebulae
nebulae and noises

I dreamt that my eyeballs
dropped out of my head

and rolled about on their own
in the waves of the ocean –
they came back to me greener

I dreamt my bones came apart
right out of my body
and danced a jig
at the top of a snowy mountain –
they came back to me whiter and stronger

since then, I can dance
and I feel quite at ease
in a total life-and-death stance.

2.
Here's a trip I often make

I go south to start with
climb up the big mountain
then come down to the red desert
no crow could cross it
I cross it, singing

I come to another big mountain
its summit all littered with bones
I pay no heed at all
I keep on travelling

after that mountain, a sea
no way over, but look, there's a bridge
only a hair's-breadth wide
have to watch your step
a lot of bones at the bottom of that sea too

so I come to a huge house
at the door, a fierce dog (*grr, grr*)

I slip by him, softly, softly
and stand before the king of the dead

when he sees me, the old man cries:
horned-beasts can't get this far
feathered beasts can't get this far
how come a little squirt like you
got this far?!
I'm a shaman, says I
OK, he says, what you want?

3.
This time
I'm going under the sea

down, down, down
I have to let the journey go

troubled waters

blue waters
green waters
troubled, troubled

hard to breathe
hard to
breathe

I'm on the back of a diver
and we've come down plunging down
into the deep sea-world

here's a cave
a cave full of seaweed
in it a woman
a beautiful woman
she's the lady of the fish

now I'm returning to the surface

sploosh!

4.
This morning
took a trip to the Big Sky

at the red sky
had a fight with a bear

at the yellow sky
had a talk with a wolf

at the green sky
looked a snake in the eye

at the blue sky
swam about with a whale

at the white sky
danced with a crane

up at the Big Sky
I'm flying round like a goose
in the absolute light

hey! hey! hey!

5.
I beat on the drum
and the birds come
the birds fly all around me
hear their wings!

now the gull talks through me
ka kayagaya ka!
now the crow

kra krarak krarak!
now the heron
fraak fraak fraak
now the great white goose
kaigaikak kaigaikak!

I dance the bird dance
look at my wings!
I fly from place to place
wings firm in the wind
higher and higher I go
with the great sea-eagle
with the wild-eyed gannet

higher up, ever higher
now I'm nothing but a moving silence.

The Gannet Philosophy

Everytime I go down to the shore, I see it: an ancient gannet, ugly as Socrates and with a very chilly eye, wings firm in the wind.

It was this grotesque angel that, years ago, led me away from frequented paths and roads – into a great emptiness, where the wind is shamanistic, and cold bites the bone.

Up in that white world, existence seemed difficult, if not impossible – till, gradually, I became acclimatized, naturalized, recognizing that others had known these regions before me, and that there was even a culture, however scattered, however obscure, attached to them, growing from them. An extreme culture, full of a hard beauty that had never run to waste, firmly grounded and yet winged.

When Nietzsche cries: 'let every body become a dancer and every spirit a bird', he is calling for white world culture. And when the Zen master says: 'the place of the spirit is nowhere, it's like the tracks of birds in the sky', he is referring to the white world, and the way to it, which is the bird-path.

1.
Way up north
where the great wind blows
he is walking

way up north
where the dawn-light breaks
he is walking

way up north
in the difficult land
he is walking.

2.
The more I walk
this northern coast

the closer I am to the East

though I bear the soil of Europe
in my bones

it is an eastern light I see
striking these stones.

3.
The white hills
have perfect reflections

I came through Lochaber
in the dead of winter

to meet Matsuo Bashô
on the Island of Dogs.

4.
All poetry comes
from facing a loveliness

all love comes
from living in nakedness

all naked life
comes from the nothingness.

5.
Let your poem
be as the gannet's wing

with power and clarity

in its wheeling

bearing erotic flesh
to the ecstasy of being.

Tractatus Cosmo-Poeticus

Take it from Hume
forgetting the human
at least the all-too-human

'the field is the world'

from the sharp lines of sceptical Scotland
move on, say, to

an ice-field in the vicinity of Reykjavik
a high plateau in Utah
a raked zen garden in Kyoto
the house of Wittgenstein in Vienna

the *tractatus logico-philosophicus*
has this:
'a picture presents a situation
in logical space
the existence and non-existence
of states of affairs'

the mind loves elements
related to one another
in a determinate way
and from there reaches out
to the sum-total of reality

forms and void
bulk and blanks

it is difficult
to avoid drawing distinctions and conclusions
so pleasant
to enter an area
beyond the climate of opinion

and over-particularized existence
where the less you say
the more is said

I think of a room in Otterthal
and snow drifting
across a silent window frame.

Letter from Harris*

> 'Although I compose poetry, I do not
> think of it as composed poetry'
> (Saigyo)

1.
The degree of isolation
is higher here
than in most places.

2.
'The ancient foreland
is continued
in the islands of the Outer Hebrides
which mainly consist
of lewisian gneiss
a metamorphic rock
over 2 000 million years old

These islands
stretch for a distance
of some 150 miles
along the west coast of Scotland
and are exposed
to the full force
of the Atlantic waves and weather.'

3.
Rodel
where the young men
built the beautiful ship
that the sea coveted
and the 'great cleric' lived

who founded the grammar school in Paris
Rodel this evening
is an empty harbour
a rusty iron ring
and a heap of red seaweed.

4.
I asked the old woman
if she liked it here
she answered:
'I'm here whether I like it or not'
and asked about the life she said:
'£1.50 a score of herring
£40 a ton of coal
14p. a loaf of bread.'

5.
I open the book
and the words
fly out of the page:
    faoileann
            annlag mhara
      bòdhag
           breac-an-t-sìl
– as I listen to them talking
the remaining ones
I hear their phrases
twining and intertwining
like carving on a stony crypt
or like the glorified lines
of a precious manuscript...

6.
But when I walk alone
the rocks or the machair
the silence itself is illuminate
and I do not think of culture
or even of subsistence
the question in my mind
is of going outward
always farther outward
to the farthest *line of light*.

7.
Phone re boat
Mr Nicholson. Grimsay. 0870-2380
Millar Mundie. 2 Floddabay. 83-234

'Calum Iain McCorquodale
might be able to take you
but I cannot
give you his phone number

I believe he has the phone now
but his number
is not yet in the book
anyway
you go and see him
and if he's going out
he'll take you
and If he's not going out
too bad'

Ronald MacDonald of Pabblesgarry
Angus Cunningham, *The Saphire.*

8.
The thousand shimmerings
this morning the sea of the monks
is a thousand shimmerings.

9.
'We think
of these northern islands
as storm-bound and mist-wrapped
yet nowhere
can there be greater
brilliance of colour
the sea so blue
the rocks so vivid
with saffron lichen

a meadow of sea pink
in June
contains all colours
between white and deep purple
and the white-feathered birds
reflect the boreal intensity
of the summer light.'

10.
Medusae
on the white sand beach:
colour of brandy and whisky
or again
infinitely pale –
like the first clutch of living jelly
in a darwinian dawn.

11.
'The disciple
sits for long hours
silent and motionless

till he enters
a state of impassivity
free of all thoughts

finally departing from the self
he penetrates
the domain of emptiness.'

12.
A guillemot
reflected
in the glassy water

shatters its image.

13.
In the room of roaring waves.

The Region of Identity

> '... before all my arrogant poems the real Me stands
> yet untouched, untold, altogether unreached'
> (Whitman)

It was evening when I got to that beach, after a couple of hundred miles hitching – the time to find a suitable place to lay out my sleeping-bag (in the lee of a drifted, sea-bleached treetrunk), and just to sit there listening to the tide and watching the stars come out, till I turned in. During the night there was a storm, a theatre of amber and blue electricity away down the horizon, with rain coming across the sea in squalls. When I woke, the sky was miraculously clear, and I had that whole coast, ten or twelve miles of it unbroken, all to myself. I started walking...

1.
How many forms discarded
        how many selves destroyed
     how many dawns and darknesses
      until I reach
          this place of light and emptiness
   where white birds cry
         a presence –
     or still yet only sign?

2.
So much life lived
     for this one flame
   so much travelling
      for this one point –
the intelligence trembles
     at the approach of naked being.

3.
The hard path of the spirit
        leads to these places
    all powerful feeling
            leads to these emptinesses
        the destiny of words
            to these moving silences.

4.
Or still yet only sign? –
      to cover my naked body
  with signs
    and be a sign among signs
    or to go beyond signs
  into the light
        that is not the sun
     into the waters
         that are not the sea.

5.
Always the metaphysical landscape
        but more and more abstract
    yet more abrupt
          where the farthest of unrealities
     are the reality
   and life
       that dancing flurry
  that line of white
      that incandescent edge
        advancing
      beyond meaning and problem.

6.
Metaphysical?
        – the physical absolute
    the opaque burned out
            the heaviness dissolved.

7.
This pool of water
      holding rock and sky
    traversed by the wing-flash of birds
          is more my original face
    than even the face of Buddha.

8.
Panic colony:
      arch-traces on the sand
    flying whiteness in the air
        the principles are here –
          my species.

9.
Cosmic body
        the cosmo-comedy.

On Bird Island

        In the northern Spring

1.
Out of the personal chaos
        the vagaries of body and mind
out of the leaves of knowledge
        cast on the wind
out of the laughing gull's throat
        and the knife-edge of its fight
out of the blaze of images
        in the black sea of night
out of the many contradictions
        as of burning ice and frozen fire
the white, the empty, the naked
        is what I desire.

2.
Here on bird island
        where the ocean breaks
in rings of white tumult
        round the fractured rocks
where the mind travels high
        on the wings of the gull
or knows a quietness
        in the curve of a shell
I have come again into my own
        the incandescence
thought reduced almost to nothing
        lost in the immanence.

Cryptology of Birds

'The teaching consists in meditating again
and again upon the bird'
(Hamsa Upanishad)

1. *Sula bassana*

Old whitehead philosopher
with a fishy beak
and a crazy eye

the way you squawk
means more than all the talk.

2. *Fulmaris glacialis*

The cool path of your flight
puts a silence in the world

buddha of the ice.

3. *Larus canus*

Common as hell
the evangel bird

watch it on any shore
writing on air, sand and water.

4. *Hydrobates pelagicus*

That's a mere sign:

but the stormy petrel
is a violent act of flesh
a violent wing-beat
from horizon to ecstatic horizon

disclosing being.

5. *Larus ridibundus*

Beyond the immobile silence
hah!

that laugh in the air.

The Bird Path

> In the northern ocean is a fish...
> This fish changes into a bird...
> It's at the time of the great tides that
> the bird leaves for the southern ocean.
> (Chuang-tzu)

1. *Of Childhood*

Raised on stilts
above the tide-line
the boats stood
like eyeless birds
bodies encrusted
with salt and shells.

2. *Of the City*

Once I lived in that city:

haar on my window
a crazy light

men with red dreams
in dark corners

a girl brought
the evangel of sex

I studied
the language of dawn.

3. *Of Studies*

It was Bhartrihari who said
that grammar leads to beatitude

I've cut the pages, hold it in my hand

open it, and see the black script stand

like the marks a drunken gannet
might leave on the sand.

4. *Of the Territory*

Up here in the white country

any tree for a totem
any rock for an altar
discover!

this ground is suicidal

annihilates everything
but the most essential

poet – your kingdom.

5. *Of the Emptiness*

This is the cold island

lying on the bare stones
gulls crying in the mist –

the immensity of nothing
empties the veins and bones.

6. *Of the Way South*

Among the dark sand
and the rosy seaweed

the deep-curved
sea-white clam shell –

she is scattered
over all the earth.

7. *Of the Pine Country*

Pinetrees
slender-trunked pinetrees
slender dark-tufted pinetrees
slender dark-tufted rain-glistening pinetrees

resin
dripping slowly
from their rosy slits.

Haiku of the Sud-Express

> 'With regard to a unity in life, art, and mental attitude, there is no other artist for whom it is so harmonized as for the haiku poet'
> (Santei)

1.
North-South, East-West
this man's identity
is difficult.

2.
Watching the frost-world
while my two fellow travellers
talk about management.

3.
Thinking of my old room:
the cup with the broken handle
that became a bowl.

4.
Further back still:
white sun shining
on the stones of the moor.

5.
A railway-cabin flashes by
I hear my father
whistling in the silence.

6.
Running around
in crazy circles
a young dog in the snow.

7.
Three cities
would take several tellings
I laugh to myself.

8.
Midday or thereabouts
I eat my rough biscuits
with a lot of saliva.

9.
Field after field
my eyes can't see
enough of this whiteness.

10.
Sun reflected
in ice over running water
this joyless joy.

11.
Snow drifting
this man's identity
is very simple.

Interpretations of a Twisted Pine

>'Learn of the pine from the pine'
>(Matsuo Bashô)

1.
I started off
by growing up
like everybody else.

2.
Then I took

a bend to the south
an inclination east
a prolongation north
and a sharp turn west.

3.
Now, approaching me
be prepared for grotesquerie

there are more than pines in my philosophy.

4.
Yes I'm something more than a pine
I'm a cosmological sign.

5.
I'm idiomatic
I'm idiosyncratic

I'm pre-socratic.

6.

I'm maybe Chinese too

like Li Po, Tu Fu
and Mr Chuang-tzu.

7.

I live quietly
but storms visit me

I do a metaphysical dance
at the heart of existence.

8.

The branches of my brain
are alive to sun and rain

my forest mind
is in tune with the wind

there is reason in my resin.

9.

Behold the mad pine
stark on the sky-line.

Remembering Gourgounel

Abandoned house, abandoned soil
walls tangled in thorns and vines
who'd waste energy on land like this
could work it years and no return
but here's a stranger, God knows why
pitching in to clear the rubble and ruck
sweat trickling down his brow and back

Old mulberries that still bear leaves
though some are on their last legs
gutted out and all out of shape
hanging on crazily to the sunburned slope
bees nesting in them, honey gathers
leave 'em where they are then, even the wrecks
they're still in touch with spinning girls

Hacking out a path among the whin
metal of mattock sparking rock
hot flies buzzing around my sweat
blue mist far away down the valley
sun throbbing fiercely in empty sky
a hawk circles quietly over the wood
snake slithers into matted grass

Goat's cheese from the neighbouring stead
and apricots fresh from this morning's tree
with rose-coloured wine from a trappist cell –
I lie still here among thorn and bramble
cool in the shadow at my midday meal
watching blue smoke rising from the western hill
and white cloud sailing over Thunder Mountain

The smith has wrought me a handy axe
just the length I need for swinging
now up in the dark wood cutting rafters
clean axe-head neatly lopping branches
then piling together tumbled stones
will have to learn how to build up walls
make a good job of that old tower

Work over, down to the hillside stream
clear water splashing by the little fall
wash myself enjoying the water's feel
seeing the dragonflies skimming the pool
darkblue-winged in the evening glow
and butterflies like fluttering petals
all the colours of the rainbow

Long hours at night beside the lamp
studying the ten books gathered here
stars clustered thick at the little window
wind soughing coolly in the chestnut wood
a rat scuttles overhead in search of grain
my eyes settle down on the page again
that bird cry is the early dawn.

Cape Breton Uplight

Just off Cape Breton, the sea, which elsewhere round the shores of Britain and France remains at the level of the continental plateau, plunges directly to oceanic depths of 5,000 metres and more, once inhabited by some of 'the big fish God created': whales. On these fecund grounds, the area seemed a good place to settle in and work with for a while. Always the search for the place and the formula, the essential locality and the few necessary words.

1.
Is there
 anywhere on the dwindling earth
 a man like me
 walking at the edge of the sea
 and...

2.
Blue shingle
 smooth pebble
 dune-grass
 express only the essential
 fix the mind.

3.
White-blow of the waves
 confused beginnings
 dissolution and amplitude
 the emptiness is plenitude
 and the gulls
 raise their spontaneous cries.

4.
Osprey
    gannet
        white-arsed petrel
    pelagians and hyperboreans
        tantric gulls
on this ascetic shore
        the abandoned ground
we haunt.

5.
Inland
        the lack of reality
    the reduction of spirit
        is ugly and wearisome
    the mind rots
        language decays
under cypher and strident opinion
        raised up as reason
the earth disappears
        from the minds of the living
the real word is lost.

6.
At the edge of the world
        in the emptiness
    maintaining the relations
        the primordial contact
            the principles by which
    reality is formed
        on the verge of the abstract.

7.
And always the question
>	is of unifying
>   simplifying
>		penetrating.

8.
Are the waters female?
>	or is woman a coastline
>	moulded by the wind?
>			walk here girl
where everything
>		answers your nakedness
>	eye and sex
>			washed in these elements
>		and the cry of your body
at one with the cry of the gulls.

9.
This morning
>	the coast is transparent
>	and the highest reaches
>			of the mind
>	are in their element.

10.
The violence of poetry
>		is still
>			and goes deep –
>	to the bone
>			to the white.

11.
Many images blur the mind
    the highest poetry
        is stricken
      with poverty of image
  when the white light
        is at its blindingest
  all objects disappear
      the skull like a sun.

The Bhodi Notebook*

In the southern Spring

1.
Little japanese apple-tree
saying quietly:
no need to go to Kyoto.

2.
Over the grasses
two white butterflies
fluttering by whitely.

3.
Old Hakuin
listening to the snow
out there at Shinoda.

4.
What's that? What's that?
the moon
reflected in my soup.

5.
Dark, dark
a sudden flash of light
illuminates the yellow whin.

6.
Young mountain peak
take off that shirt of mist
so I can see your snowy nakedness.

7.
Me and my silence
drinking tea together –
how are things, boy?

8.
Another presence
in the empty room –
ah! the rain.

9.
All those teachings –
the summit, O.K.
the rest, my own way.

River*

1. Biography

From the black mountains it comes
the land of memory and meteors

when
in the Causse Country
it flows over chalky rock
it seems to want to go back
curling in on itself
in long dark meanders

opening out then, superbly
it crosses the most fertile plain of France

so as to meet, after the Garonne

the ocean.

2. The Movement of Long Thought

Lingeringly, dreamingly
the river moves across the territories

in the white dawn silence
in the grey mist of evening

under smoking showers

with long clear stretches
over shining stones

the lover of long thought
could not walk along a river
without tears in his eyes.

3. Three Moments

In the mist of evening
a grey heron
flying over the reeds.

*

You can't even see his shadow
but he's there
the kingfisher.

*

Between a question and a question
between a silence and a silence
the river's murmuring.

The Wild Swan Scroll

It came out of a studio at the Porte des Lilas
by an artist from Hanchow
long resident in France

it was a map and it was a territory
but also the body of the swan itself
dark and white-grey and frosty blue
with here and there a rosiness as of sun on snow

the paint had flowed and the flight was written
all the long lines of the migration
with ridges and gullies clearly marked
lakes and valleys
and the courses of meandering rivers

it was beautiful and it was full of meaning
at once a testament and a testimony
to all that China ever thought of landscape
yet it was not Chinese

the artist had read through all the histories
followed bird-tracks in all the poetries
and studied the documents of science
but mostly through long years of silence
she had listened to the music of the earth

it was a song of the earth, no swan-song
no symbol, no myth disturbed the flow
it was the song of the earth and a silence
an image of all that the mind could ultimately know.

Memories of Silver River

According to erudite authorities, the name of the Loire can be traced right back to Egypt. Ausonius sang of the Moselle in rolling Latin lines. In grandiloquent paragraphs, Victor Hugo praised the Rhine. Compared to those impressive waterways, my little Silver River is poor and insignificant – but so lovable. I'm not going to drown it in floods of rhetoric, or load it with a treatise on potamology. Let's just try and quietly follow its meanderings, get in touch with some of its intimate movements, see its flickering lights. The poetics suitable for the Silver River is riverwriting, water-verse, with maybe, now and then, a little hydrological haiku.

1.

Very few know the river's source

ask any citizen resident in the region
all they do is stare

but the river remembers:

dark rock
the smell of earth
the first Spring rain.

2.

The Argens never forgets its tributaries:

the Caramy
the Nartuby
the Riberotte
the Issole

all together
taking their time
they mingle with the sea at St Raphaël.

3.

There are rivers
that have three beds

a normal bed
an extraordinary bed
a middling bed

the Argens has one, only one
it keeps its head.

4.

Yet there are years
around September's third week
when, heavy with summer heat
she uses a sudden autumnal downpour
to flood her banks

a depression centred on Aquitania
doesn't leave her cold
an anticyclone
somewhere over Eastern Europe
can touch her to the quick.

5.

If she delights in summer
the Argens likes it also when skies are grey

they keep fools away

on those grey days
she's alone, all alone

with her reeds and her willows.

6.

While claiming to be
the lords of the earth
those poor human creatures
feel such existential dearth
(closed up in their identity
they feel lost, utterly lost
in the vastness of eternity)
that the river accepts with grace
the way they carve their names all over the place –
but as for her
friend of stone and abyss
she flows on, fundamentally anonymous.

7.

There was a time
when fish abounded here

eel
roach
ablet
char
barbel
salmon-trout

what about today ?

(the best source
for fishy information
is the Great Cormorant
who's been around since the Creation).

8.

We could pile up a lot of statistics
about this little river
turning it into
a most complicated entity

but what the river by far prefers
is just to flow on and on and on
in total complexity.

9.

When her movement
gets even stiller than you could imagine
the old man who roams her banks
attentive to her every mood
says:
'Quiet, now, quiet
the river is lost in thought.'

Scenes of a Floating World*

Hong Kong Bay, 1975

1.
A warm white mist over the bay
and an old junk making it
the slow way –
something would like this quietness to stay...
but already it's day: cranes turning,
people scurrying, engines chugging,
sirens howling, phones ringing
– and Hong Kong wakens to more money-making.

2.
Fish market look-see:
the red sun glistens
on big-eyes, bream, manta rays
shark, barracuda, sea-snake
while blue smoke rises from joss-sticks
lit by bone-weary fishermen
in thanks for Queen of Heaven's bounty
and safe home-coming into Fragrant Harbour.

3.
Sounds of Cantonese
and a confusion of yellow faces
(Hong Kong side – Kowloon side)
the ferry-boat open to the wind
crosses the green strait
amid junks, walla-wallas, launches:
red and black print of newspaper
and a whiff of the South China Sea.

4.
She's a private secretary
('how private', she asked when she got the job)
twenty years old, pretty as a picture (no plastic surgery)
makes about $3,000 (H.K.) a month
has a flat to herself in Happy Valley
mistress to a rich local doctor
and dreams of being a student in Hawaii –
crossing the ferry 'in the morning time'.

5.
The old black Mongolian beggar
comes down from his roost
in the Kowloon hills
long-haired, laughing to himself
walking the pavement with naked feet
leaving a trail of emptiness
a long trail of laughing emptiness
that goes back to Cold Mountain.

6.
In the airconditioned skyscraper office
a thousand cases of Mexican abalone
come in on one line
and a ton of Chinese rabbits
leave on another – while in the backstreets
old men play noisy mahjong
among the guff of frying titbits, the stench
of decaying vegetables, and the ghostly smell of incense.

7.
In his cluttered little premises on Mody Street
Bossie Wong, alias Édouard (British passport, Mauritian
    French, Chinese)

waits for his next batch of clients
ready to supply them with suits, cases, watches – you name it
and offering his famous underworld mystery tour
with flower-boats and darkened omnibus
where you can feel up a nude little neighbour
for so much every five minutes.

8.
Lying at his ease
stretched out against a pillar at Kowloon Pier
Ken Cameron, vagrant
opens the *South China Morning Post*
reads the speech made by a British general
at a rotary club dinner –
then turns to the many-dated shipping page
looking for a likely boat.

9.
With two new film-scripts under his arm:
'The Canton Killers', 'Murder in Macao'
(guaranteed 100% commercial success)
white-suited moustachio'd Brooklyn Joe
walks up Nathan Road in the blue afternoon
while the young model practises smoking the cigarette
that makes her sick
('We are Hong Kong people, no politics').

10.
Scott Hawkins, writer
having travelled all Asia
sits in his hotel room in Tsimshatsui
a bottle of whisky at his elbow
and a newly bought notebook before him –

on the notebook's first page is inscribed
'The Face of the East Wind'
below that: 'an impossible novel'.

11.
At nightfall, the streets are strident
with neon signs, black
dance of ideograms; a blond-haired Dutch girl
shows clammy breasts to Japanese tourists
in a smoky cellar; a Filipina girl does the same
for beer-happy Yankee sailors
while bulldog British businessman is daintily escorted
by a tongue-tied little Hongkongese.

12.
Kowloon Kino:
peeled oranges at the entrance
chestnuts roasting in charcoal
sputtering chicken, meatballs, tripe –
inside the huge hall
your neighbour puffs like a maniac and spits on the stone floor
while bones crunch, blood spurts
and heroines whimper on the giant screen.

13.
In his tenth floor flat
in the backlands
laid out Japanese style with mats
but with a Chinese *pi-pa* in one corner
Christopher Cheung
('I am not an artist, I am a human being')
pours himself a glass of *maotai*
 and dreams of Kyoto.

14.
In the bar near 2 o'clock closing-time
Oscar Eberfeld, bachelor, 46 years old
eyes with hopeless desire
the little slit-skirted serving-girl
follows a wench on the pavement
glued to the knicker-line showing through her pants
then returns unconsoled to his room
with a glossy magazine.

15.
Over in Aberdeen
a satisfied rat slides home
under the floor of a waterfront restaurant
the last gamblers yawn and spit
the last sampan putters in to anchorage –
while two heavy-beamed stern-high junks
plough the dark harbour
bound for ancient fishing-grounds.

Mahāmudrā*

>'When the mind finds no place to stop,
>there is mahāmudrā.'
>(Mahāmudrāpādesha)

1.
Northwards again
'you come and go, you come and go'
red leaves along the waterways
quiet walking in the rain

feeling your body
growing out of the rain

then into the museum

my ten cents in the machine
the raga mingling with the rain

ah, now

your body in the dance
the red mark on your brow.

2.
Out of India
'beautiful as a mare from Kashmir'

'eyes like silver fish'
long crowblack hair
firm dark round breasts

and the navel's lonely pool

all that I knew of India
all that I knew
centred in your body

surasundarī
realising the wave
beyond the ambiguities of love.

3.
For years you had followed your path
and I mine
(mine the more erratic –
but *pratyātmavedaniya*
'left to individual')
you with a master
me with a madness

'how can men of this age
of restless mind and lax intelligence
prone to distraction
attain to purity of disposition?'

the search among books
the moments the flashes
the encounters

seeing in every girl *prajñā*

the one aim : *samarasa*
achieved through aimlessness.

4.
Glasgow:
incandescent limbo
in my student's room
with the *sūtra* and *tantra*
listening to India through the wall
(three engineers from New Delhi

modern discs spun for hours on end
smell of smoke-perfume in the hall)
and the waiter in the Tajmahal:
'my soul is shaking in my belly...
my heart is anxious... for my girl
who plays... the flute' –
kitsch out of Bombay
1960

on the suspension bridge
at twilight
the blue sari.

5.
With the word-master in Paris
'useless conversations'
the Bamboo Grove

'*le Zen c'est de la connerie
mais les Shingon
ça c'est des gars carabinés*'

lodging rue des Écoles
ten books a week
the ocean of learning

'the white peaks of the Himalaya'

linking it all
to a few root images
all truth ultimately
within the body
the body-mind
word flesh image bone

'the inarticulate heart's true tone'.

6.
'As soon as the conscience
is rid of its covering
it stands out naked
and energy shows its essence'

the lotus and the lightning

'just as salt is dissolved in water
so the mind that takes its woman'

in the arms of the knowledge-girl

earth water fire wind
and space too – honour them

'so he comes into relation
with every kind of creature
and knows the path of freedom'.

7.
Now the long-hidden Real
within the names and forms

the moment when
twenty thousand breathings
reach their plenitude

'rain also is of the process'

and the music
       and the dancing body

abhisambhodi

it all whirls incessantly
under the laws of change
but there is light in it

there is a rain of light
flooding the brain

'a pure flow of consciousness
a stream of colourless emotion'.

The House of Insight

> 'Developing insight is like diving
> into the deep waters of sensation'
> (Nagasena, *Vipassana*)

I saw myself disappearing
and it was good
for I was still there
another

eliminate the intermediary me

I was Gauguin
I was a Chinese scholar

totally relaxed
plenitudinous reality

oh girl bellygirl lovely brightmoving girl

coming
always coming
and be-coming

you think it's over
another lovely wave comes

undisturbed
the secret sequence

physics of being
physics of writing
all one

words
like 'em, lick 'em, lip 'em

suck valley dark furry valley
dark furry flurry
slick lick
slit little slit soogling so sucking
lubbery lips lipping

to be into something
ingoing knowing

combinations
aware of 'em happening
with all my senses

red rut in the golden body
dark in the gold
raw red in the dark gold

making love to the unknown

salmon in the falls
the long green moss caress
the fur-patch touch

did that fellow know what he was saying?
know thyself

silky emptiness
silky silky emptiness

knowing things in the deep pleasure-core

a wet day in the woods
with all senses flush

whale thing pring sling
pale slap slip
spill spale swale whale

a whole white space
we haven't got into yet

the white of a milky wave

everything so absolutely
beautifully clear

beyond images
the fire-body
live from the fire-body

never mind subject-object
get into the rhythm

polyrhythmic delight
nothing to do with music
music only makes a noise about it

something else
trying to light up
at the back of my skull

getting down to the wave and pulse level

maybe deep down
we live this way all the time
but we don't know it
our consciousness isn't alive to it

our consciousness
is full of social noise

I could probably invent a mathematics
but my mind is in love
with another kind of truth

the flow doesn't really want
philosophies or science
it wants you
to get into the flow

stop worrying at the world

all those dogmas
all that back-biting
all that anxiety

ah!
the long morning of the mind

smoke dancing
birds flying
river flowing

seeing into it
and feeling it all out

there's no essence
only multi-movement

swirling joyance

she-territory
wave-world

moving among the unnamed

in-being
fields of in-being

no wishful thinking

philosophy's holiday
an ontological vacation

no paradise
but to move in a multiple
paradoxical field

glow-flow

silent

listen

two powers meeting
smile at each other

sun rising
over white flesh ridge
rain of golden fire

fire-body
not the old doll
in the conceptual dustbin

eroto-logic

that's very neat
came to me straight from the Paraclete

multiple meditations
the wonderful understanding
wunderstanding

into the nakedness
behind the signs

deep deep down
where it all
ultimately matters

anonymous conscience
anonymous contact

body-mind beautiful

two jumps ahead
and lightning in the brain

surrounded by eternity.

    (A smoky evening on the banks of the Mekong)

The Eight Eccentrics*

China, in the Tao times

1.

They say I feed on the wind
and drink dew
that's true – some of the time
but now and again
you'll find me in a village tavern
drinking rice wine
and eating fish
served by a pretty young waitress
then
after taking a good look around
listening to how the people talk
(always the same old crap)
I come back up into the hills

to follow the way of the white clouds.

2.

I'm the one does everything all mixed up
and backside foremost

when I go into town
I put a shoe on one foot
and leave the other bare

that gives people a laugh
and gets the conversation going

up in the mountains
I like sprawling naked in the snow
reading the *Autumn Waters*

when the notion comes over me
I get up on the back of a white crane
and do some celestial sight-seeing

if you see what I mean.

3.

I used to go
for long walks in the country
thinking about the Way...

one day I came across
two old raggedy fellows
who said:
– What do you think you're doing, boy?
– I cultivate the Way
– Where's the Way? they said
I pointed up to heaven
– Where's heaven? they said
I pointed to my heart
they laughed, the two of them
and said:
– OK, come away with us.

4.

Property?
ten thousand acres of white cloud
culture and the arts?
the wind in the pines

you can sit on a cushion and meditate
till you're blue in the face
you'll never know the real way of things
when people ask me to explain the Way
I just point to the sun and the moon.

5.

They say I had a white mule
that could travel a thousand miles a day
which is all baloney

it's true I had a grey mule for a while
but it went to the mules' paradise
before very long
and mostly I went about on foot
liked it better that way

people don't really care for the mountain life
prefer security and boredom
so they sit at their hearths
and make up stories
to make it all sound marvellously impossible.

6.

I was making for the capital
to sit the civil service exam
when I had that dream

I'd come out well
I had an important post
I had a wife and a son and a daughter
then my wife took a lover
war broke out
my son was killed my daughter carried off
I had to take to the hills
living on nothing

when I woke up
I decided I might as well
come up into the hills right away

so I did
and this unofficial existence

suits me down to the ground

I prefer pinetrees to politicians.

7.

As a young man they told me
I'd better undertake some serious studies
I told them I didn't want to study
all the dreary stuff they went in for
and I wrote them this poem:

'I'll live in the woody mountains
in a cave beside a waterfall
I'll play the Green Jade Song
on a seven-stringed lute
I'll grow a magic mushroom or two
and feed them to a snow-white crow'

I've lived like that
for close on fifty years
now I'm lying here under a pure autumn sky
with a smile on my face.

8.

I never wanted to be president
of the company, or the country
I wanted to be what I read in the old books
'a real man without situation'

you don't often come across fellows like me
here today and gone tomorrow
following the ten directions of the heart

home for me is a hillside cave
out on one of the Eastern Islands
don't think I live a sad life there
I drink white wine and let my soul
fly about with the gulls.

BOOK V

Mountain Meditations

The Pyrenean years. Distance and silence, heights and depths. I tended to equate the mountains with 'the perfection of wisdom' (*prajnaparamita*). That's what they were on the horizon. But I also spent a lot of time moving through them, from cave to crest. The greatest abstraction needs the crudest reality. From the mountains I began gradually moving again along the coast.

Pyrenean Passage

1. To the South-West
I'd written to Le B.
Professor at the Sorbonne
(author of an *Anthology of American Poetry*
and a deadly series of detective novels)
whom I'd known when I was a *lecteur* there
asking him if he might know of a job for me
preferably outside Paris
somewhere in what were still called 'the provinces'

he wrote back saying he had a post for me in the big city
as to the provinces, well
young assistants I had come in contact with
there in the Rue de l'École-de-Médecine
had scattered all over the hexagon:
L. was at Rouen
S. at Pau
E. at Nice

I wrote to all three

at Nice, there was nothing doing
but from Rouen and Pau
came positive replies
I weighed them up carefully
decided Rouen was climatically too close to Glasgow
and chose Pau

'Pau (64000)
cap. of the Béarn
admin. centre of the Pyrénées-Atlantiques
on the *gave* of Pau
751 km S.-W. of Paris
pop. 85766 (Palois).'

2. **Villa Formosa**

I'd been wandering for years in the fogs of Glasgow
still in its late industrial phase
(gulls wailing over the Clyde's dirty waters
a hundred wastelands)
reading Spengler and Toynbee
Eliot and Thomas de Quincey
who had lived in the Rottenrow
up on the city's old hill
beside Kentigern's cathedral...

at the top of another hill
(Gilmorehill, the University quarter)
I'd started up the Jargon Group
doing talks and poetry readings
(in churches, in the philosophy amphitheatre)
publishing pamphlets
that were relayed from London
by the para-situationist Sigma Centre
to a band of people all over the world
including Ronald Laing, the 'anti-psychiatrist'
and *Naked Lunch* Burroughs in Tangiers

Pau, at that time, didn't have a university
it had a '*collège littéraire*'
linked to Bordeaux
housed in the Villa Formosa
near the Allées de Morlaas

while ostensibly and officially
teaching 'English language and literature'
I was in reality delving into
culture-analysis
and the question of expression

I started up the *Groupe Feuillage*
thinking of Whitman
('Always our old feuillage
always the free range and diversity')
talking about a Creative University

ready to begin again from Pau(manok)

the group grew
the little magazine *Feuillage* began to flutter in the breeze

this was the Autumn of '67 and the Winter of '68

when the month of May came
I listened like everybody else to the news from Paris
and read the literature

I had no faith at all in the movement of May
then, as now
I could only believe in some long-term policy
but at least this was a clout in the face of complacency
so I had to go with it

that meant issuing tracts
organizing meetings
manifesting in various ways

so that, if before
I was poet and outsider
now to those who were convinced they had authority
I became sheer anathema

in June I was told
my contract would not be renewed
some people even thought
I'd been 'invited' to leave the country for good

'The university doesn't need brilliant minds'
declared a Palois professor
(whose conception of British civilization
was London clubs, the Royal Family and the Derby)
thereby complimenting me with the left hand
while throwing me out with the right

well, the June air was bright

I raised my eyes to the hills.

3. **The Tower, 1969**

The Résidence d'Aspin had wide windows
in them, the line of the Pyrenees
from the Pic du Midi de Bigorre over to the Pic d'Anie

they became my mental horizon

I took out some old books
(among them German treatises on philology)
and bought some new ones

reading studies
comparing Euskara to Suomi and Magyar
ugro-altaic languages in general
with Charency, for example
trying to push the Basques back
to Eastern Europe at least
if not to farthest Asia

it's true that *churia* (yellow) and *gorria* (red)
seem close to Buriat *shara* (yellow)
and Japanese *shira* (white)

I imagined
a centre of brightness
radiating out over the territories...

I read about place-names
around the Gave de Pau and the Gave d'Oloron
non-Roman
who knows, maybe even non-Indo-European:

Gabas, Artouste, Ibos
Osse, Asté, Aubisque
Navarrenx, Orthez, Béost...

singular phonetics
archetypal topographies

signs of Aquitanian resistance
in the extreme South-West
and the high mountain valleys

gabarro: gorse
gabardéro: wild rose
arrèc: stream
arriang: vulture
gango: mountain crest
garrinera: line of rocks
labardàu: torrent

I read Bosch-Gimpera : *Los Celtas y el país vasco*

I read Paulinus, who, over in the Médoc
(Aquitania, the same word as Guyenne?)
in correspondence with Ausonius of Bordeaux
called the Pyrenees *Vasconiae Saltus*

trying to get in touch with the territory

always the love for locality
outside all the localisms.

4. In the Café of the Reine Marguérite

Autumn in the South-West

still dark, eight o'clock
(Marie-Claude leaves at seven-thirty for the lycée at Lourdes)
sitting in the Café of the Reine Marguérite
on the square of the same name
rain falling...

I'll stay here quiet for an hour
before making another little reconnaissance
in the streets of Pau

listening to conversations at the market
'hilh de pute...'
picking up a little volume or two
in some second-hand bookshop

thinking this morning of Gaston Phébus
born April 1331 at Foix
who, inheriting that Languedoc county
as well as Gascon lands to the West
(Béarn, Marsan, Gabardan)
and a part of the Nébouzan around Saint-Gaudens
was out to create in the Pyrenees
an autonomous region
able to stand up to the states of England and France

a wellnigh impossible enterprise
involving politics, economics and cultural ideas

that fellow's path was strewn with difficulty and drama

at Orthez in 1380
he stabbed to death his own son
who had tried to poison him
after which he shut himself up in the castle at Pau

writing his *Livre des Oraisons*
('Oh God, I've travelled so many roads
I think I know you')

eight years later he wrote a *Livre de chasse*
describing the woods of the South-West
as he saw them with his green and loving eyes
('Oh, beautiful are the woods
bright with dew
and luminous all these lands')

when he died in 1391
he left 730.000 florins in the coffers of Orthez
a goodly library
full of poetry, science and philosophy
and a dream
that might have left this area
with more than what you come across so frequently:
a stubbornly cultivated complacency
along with an inordinate enthusiasm for rugby

but perhaps not
maybe nothing more
than another Monaco or Andorre

it's a highly complex matter, culture
and difficult to accumulate the elements of grandeur.

5. **Barriers and Passages**

These mountains have always been
both barrier and passage

remember Hannibal
coming in against Rome over the Perthus
(elephant spoors in the pristine snow)

hence that line of frontier posts
stretched out all along the chain
from the *Portus Veneris*
to the *puntas arenas of* the West

and the carolingian marches
marca hispanica, marca hesperica

frontier fluctuations
boundary perturbations
Emperor confronting Emir
Cross clashing with Crescent
(at times strange alliances and collusions)

Frankish troops on the Southern Front
Saracen troops on the Northern Front

that famous year, 778
a cosmopolitan army
bringing together among others Bavarians and Burgundians
crosses the Pyrenees
at the Col des Albères in the East
at the Col de Roncevaux in the West

to Saragossa! to Saragossa!

in the West there, Roland
marquis of Anjou
praefaectus limitis britannici...

when the *Regnum Francorum,* the Carolingian empire
begins to collapse and crumble
the nationalisms arise
in Catalonia, for example, and Navarre:
ethnic complexes
territory and conscience
soil and soul

an old story

transcended only if at all
by those pilgrims carrying a shell
to the sanctuary in Compostella.

6. **Ossau Valley Notes**

Once, like the Aspe, a route of exchange

rising up to cols open much of the year
leading to the Rio Aragon and the region of Jaca

oceanic
open to Atlantic influence from the West and North-West
a place of wet and mist
though at times a warm dry wind
will blow up from the Spanish South

Arudy stands at the entrance
where, in a cave
were found rocks and pebbles
engraved with reindeer, horses
(little ponies still run wild in the valley)

a narrow corridor
only the bottom land turned over
upstream from Laruns, agriculture stops

serrated ridges and craggy peaks
perpetual snow at 7,000 feet
pile-ups of boulders from Ice Age rivers

at a cross-roads of ancient tracks
a dolmen

here, another
placed on a little plateau looking out to the sun

elsewhere, cromlechs
(places of tribal gathering?)
at Cabane de la Glère
at Couraïs d'Accaüs

in the early days of this century
shepherds still built stone circles round their huts

even on the heights
the best pastures in the Pyrenees
replete with liquorice
(thanks to a glacial soil that retains moisture
as well as a variety of elemental richness)

sheep bleating under the shady foliage
of Hondaas de las Hadas

the mountains resound with archaic symphonies.

7. The Flight of Jean-le-Blanc

All praise to the world of birds!

especially, here in the Pyrenees
Jean-le-Blanc

see him, over by the coomb there
swooping, skimming, gliding

cold energy incarnate
but also like some paracletian idea
emerging from the dialogue of logos and Holy Ghost
in the brilliant palaces of Byzantium
or in the caves of Cappadocia
where the stoician *amor fati*
later taken up by Nietzsche on the plateau of the Engadine
walked with a new transcendence

(*kenosis*
the spirit come down to rock and clay
amid the confusion of humanity
a relative absolute
and yet re-arising
via the Word
according to the most ancient testament of Nature)

that winged world!

out from *Archaeopteryx*
embedded in the cretacious slate of Solenhofen

there at Gargas
alongside two hundred mutilated human hands
the beautiful Aurignacian heron
thereafter, Magdalenian traces:
a goose engraved on reindeer-antler
a swan cut carefully into a pebble

evolving ever since the Eocene
crossing over boundaries and ever more invisible thresholds

their existence translated
by Boios in his *Ornithologia*
by that inveterate follower of swan-tracks
Alexander the Myndian
by Avicenna and Averroes
(who hauled us up from the ecclesiasticals' fabulous clutter
through Aristotle
back out into open and moving reality)
by Albertus Magnus (*De Animalibus*)
by Vincent de Beauvais in his *Speculum*
by Konrad von Megenburg (*Buch der Natur*)

by William Turner

Konrad Gesner
John Kay
Thomas Browne
John Ray
Christopher Merret
Martin Martin
Thomas Pennant
John Latham
George Montagu
Eleazar Albin
Gilbert White
(salutations to the world-watchers in every place!)

on to Nitzsch's *Pterylography*
and Stresemann's *Entwicklung der Ornithologie*

not forgetting John White's drawings in Virginia
Cartwright's notes from Labrador
the reports of Samuel Hearne from the North-West Territories

field knowledge
phenomena as against fantasia
and yet always the other undefined dimension

still watching
that Jean-le-Blanc

six-foot wing span
about two kilos in weight
circaetes gallicus

out for snakes and lizards
but also, I am sure
for the sheer delight in flying

swooping! skimming! gliding!

8. Between Two Seas

Like the Caucasus
the Pyrenees go from sea to sea

I see donkeys laden with heavy paniers
on the old track over the moors of Lannemezan
carrying the salt of the earth
from Dax, Accous, Salies-de-Béarn
over towards Perpignan and the ports of the Mediterranean

there was the salt-road
and there was the sea-road

Phoenician boats
sniffing their way out
beyond what the Greeks called
the pillars of Hercules
(Pindar warning: go no farther!)
into the vast Atlantic

rounding Spain
coursing along the Basque lands
watching out for the signal fire
lit on the promontory of Biarritz

then moving up farther through the mists
on the tin road to Cornwall

Pytheas thereafter
cosmographer and navigator
reconnoitering the coasts
of Europe's North-West

skirting the Celto-Iberian lands
moving up to Uxisama
from there to Cape Belerion
and on to Thule

then back to Massilia
via the home of the Hyperboreans
Scandia, Baltia
and northern Celtia

(none of those in authority
including Strabo, no dunce
believed a word he wrote)

eight centuries later
Avienus
a mind open
to geography, astronomy, meteorology
following in his imagination
the great path that goes
from the Black Sea by the Mediterranean out into the Atlantic

translating from the Greek
Phaenomena and *Prognostica*
writing in Latin his own *Ora maritima*

fascinated by migrations
and archipelagoes
and lost thalassocracies

setting out the prolegomena
of a cosmopoetical *paideuma*

days on end
in my Pyrenean studio
reading text after text
poring over *periplum* and *portolano:*
Stockler's *Origem e progressos das mathematicas em Portugal*
Memoria da vida e escritos de Pedro Nunes
by Antonio Ribeiro dos Santos

'*Manifesto he*

que estes descobrimentos de costas, ylhas e terras firmes
nam se fizeram indo a acertar
mas partiam os nossos mareantes
muy ensinados e providos do estrimentos...
levaram cartas muy particularmente rumadas'

working out my own cartography
with an enlarged and heightened conception of poetry.

9. Storm at Saint-Jean-de-Luz

The cantabrian gulf is in turmoil
likewise the sky above

the whole coast is full of noise

I hear
Franco-Spanish colloquies on the Ile-aux-Faisans
and the broken refrains of old whaling songs

while Compostellians sleep in the hostelry Esquerena
Captain Etcheverry dreams of Sumatra

meteorological manifestos!

convolutions, evolutions
of *eros, logos, cosmos*

the rhetoric of Saint-John Perse
mingles with the ravings of Hölderlin

thunder and lightning
biblical rain!

I walk along the Socoa dyke
to salute the chaos and the void

all hail, *apocalyptica*!

ocean mountains.

In Aquitania*

Prologue
'I'll show you the tombstone', he said
'no, not the tombstone, the...'

Flamen and duumvir
quaestor and district chief
Verus
having acquitted himself in Augustus' presence
of the charge that had been laid on him
obtained for the nine peoples
their separation from the Gauls –
back home from Rome
he dedicates this altar
to the genius of the place.

1.
Wind blows down from the meseta
warm rain drifts in from the ocean

fir-trees brush the snow-line
high hill beeches
hold coldness in their foliage
heather and tough grass grip the sandy edge

on flakes of sandstone
on pebbles, on fragments of bone
they draw birds and deer
and hares and horses
salmon and seals

maybe somebody
wandering in the hills
raises that shrill cry

that starts down guttural low
and winds up whinneying high.

2.

After the ice, the sea rises
rivers swollen
low valleys flooded
all along the littoral
lagoons and marshes

the coast seeping with wetness

dripping caves

people perched
on the hills and ridges

keeping watch.

3.

Basque azilian
lasts into the Atlantic phase
Maluquer speaks of a
'*vida neolítica
con una economía de recolectores*'

the face of the coast
wrapped in mist

maybe down to the shore
in winter
(red deer went down then
to feed on seaweed and
coastal grass)

a diet of deermeat and shellfish
acorns and hazelnuts.

4.

Clearing forests by burning

marsh dwellings

early words for weaving
tilling the soil
the same as in Caucasian

(old stories:
the pagans grew wheat
at the mouth of their caves)

sub-boreal, sub-atlantic

on to sheep, cattle, goats and pigs.

5.

As the Basco said:
'In the Pyrenees my father keep sheep
his father keep sheep
his father...'

those black-headed sheep
with the curling horns
that have moved
from winter to summer
between the valley
and the mountain pasture

from time immemorial

'deep are the trails
on these vales and hills.'

6.

Maybe at the beginning
the whole tribe moved
in a nomad way
then some went, some stayed:
transhumance

big stone burials
(and shelters?)

dolmens
along tracks, ridges
watersheds, crests
cromlechs higher up
windy peaks

rites (of different types?)

open views East
to catch the dawning sun
and give protection
from the westerlies.

7.

Real writing had deserted Rome
(Virgil and Ovid long gone)
it went on
in the Greek-minded cities of Provence
or, in a quieter way
here in Aquitania
where the stone world
still spoke to the ocean
and mind was open to wind

Ausonius to Theon:
'you who plough
the sandy lands of the Atlantic'

and to Paulinus:
'where the swollen waters
of the Garunna
provoke the sea'.

8.

The rhythm continued

men were there
to see to things
and draw the lines

the landscape grew

it was possible
to speak of peopled place
and cultured space

'quiet Aquitania
on the verge of Ocean'

brought forth from work
and from meditation.

9.

This morning at Grayan
I dedicate this inadequate poem
to the dune carnation

the dune carnation
little pink flower
its last home here
on these Aquitaine sands

little pink flower
carrying the whole of history
in its slender roots

a world in miniature
and religion, of a sort

destroyed
by fools on motorbikes
in the name of Sport.

The Master of the Labyrinth*

1.
'I ride in my car
I think of prehistoric caves
in the Pyrenees' –
William Carlos Williams
New York State
circa 1920.

2.
He went down there
with a smoking torch
down into
the bowels of the earth
with images of deer
bison horses
flickering in his brain
and he painted them
ecstatically
on the sweating rock.

3.
The painted cave
apocalypse of the mind.

4.
Five deer cross the mountain stream
necks outstretched, antlers
caught in the light
eyes ignoring history
cross the red ochre water
in a morning of time.

5.
Apocalypse of the mind

sex orgy
play of energy.

6.
The hunched bison
thunderous magnificent flesh
glares
at the little rag-doll
of an ichtyophallic man
while a bird-stick
planted close by
seems to say
      'signed: the shaman'.

7.
Those hands, that eye.

8.
What went on down there?
what kind of psychomental theatre?

did he smoke weird herbs in the dark?
did he get *stoned*?

9.
Sitting there petrified

body smeared
with ochre and permanganate

gazing at the wall.

10.
Then maybe, feeling horny
blowing his semen into
the crannies of the rock.

11.
Came out
sniffing the cool mountain air
reassuring all
that reality was solid
right to the centre

he'd fixed it.

Valley of Birches*

1.
Entering this valley
    is like entering a memory

        obscure the feeling
        of a plenitude lost
        about to be regained

what is this valley
    that speaks to me like a memory
whispering with all its branches
    this november morning?

2.
The wording would have to come from mental territories still unknown to me, like those phrases I sometimes wake with and that delight me with their freshness and their unstrained complexity – as when, only a few days ago, I woke with the words 'Kanaan Ross' in my mind, the strange ambiguity of the name satisfying me, and its linking of North and East. And it is as though I were now myself that Kanaan Ross, walking in this place, with the need to voice it.

3.
I must enter this birch-world
and speak from within it
I must enter into
this lighted silence

contemplation is not enough

never fully realised
without the necessary words.

4.
Without the necessary words

but the most needful words
are the rarest

and how can we come to them
maimed as we are

except through
a power that wings us

out of the maze and the din of unknowing
and enables us

to quietly
penetrate the reality –

this is no question
of industry.

5.
And yet all the work, all the research I have done is not irrelevant to this encounter. For some time now I have been studying, with a rare sense of recognition, the geography and mytho-poetry of north-east Asia, that area inhabited by the hyperborean tribes of the Chuktchee, the Buryat, the Koriak... Up in those regions, to which I feel a strong attachment, so strong they must in some sense be 'my world' , the birch-tree is sacred. Indeed the birch-tree is to the North-East what the bamboo is to countries farther south: the very heart of a culture. It is the birch-culture at the back of my mind that has given rise to my fascination with this birchwood here this morning. Like any complete culture, the birch-culture links sexuality (for the Siberian tribes the tree is the forest-girl) with the furthest reaches of the mind. Hence too the plenitude felt by me earlier, and which I maintain now deep in the dark, protecting it as it were with this prose periphery, like a bark...

6.
Waiting for the words
to come out of the silence

words for this emptiness-plenitude
this absence-presence

words for the sensual spirit
infusing those trees

words like the *nichtwesende wesenheit*
of Meister Eckhart

words like the buddhist *sunyata*
but more rooted, more rooted

rooted and branched
and running with sap.

7.
'No people knows now the sensual language', writes Jakob Böhme. Victims of concept and model, our subtle life flattened under the weight of the general, we move in sterile worlds, doing violence to everything, including ourselves. Before we can ever say anything, anything at all, we must link ourselves, by a long silent process, to the reality. Only long hours of silence can lead us to our language, only long miles of strangeness can lead us to our home.

8.
Rain falls from the blue immensities.

9.
I have come in under the trees
making love to them with my inarticulate hands

for the beauty at least may be sensed

I have traced out the black on the white
like an unfinished poem –

always broken off, always recommenced.

Crow Meditation Text*

Everybody knows
the sad sweet tale
of the nightingale
but when crow starts croaking
hard and hoarse
that's something else

crow, I tell you, is one queer Joe

crow is a ghost
he's a bird with a past

crow is king
of his own mad world
in which he's always croaking

usually
nobody listens to crow

but when one of your friends
takes off for the icelands
and writes back in a letter
about a weird crow-encounter
somewhere in the snowfields
and when a few days later
as you come through the door
of a Montparnasse apartment
the first thing you set eyes on
is a huge lump of a crow
whose croaking days are over
but looks as if it knew
a thing or two

you begin to wonder

you find yourself asking
what there is to crow

why does crow crow?
where does crow go?
what does crow know?

crow first of all
is polyglottal

crow talks double dutch
with a mixture of eskimo
russki, nahuatl
sanskrit, chinese, snohomish
as well as several brands of english

crow has been around!

Edgar Allan Poe,
was a crow

the anthropologist *enyerbado*
turned into a crow

I suppose all the Crows
were crows

I once thought of founding
an Academy of Gulls
(based on an ancient
Chinese model)
with one aim in view:
say the world anew
dawn-talk
grammar of rain, tree, stone
blood and bone

I can conceive of black gulls
and white crows
(no race fiends need apply)
I mean crow could also be
of the Gull Academy
the croaking member

but that plan went with the wind
and I ended up
with broken wings
on a cold island

smoking the weeds of my mind

anyway
the fact is
bird-men are still going around
thinking a feathered dream
croaking, yelling, squawking
all relative heavyweights
which is to say
no warbling or chirping

it's a tough world
and you have to be able
to go it through blizzards

ka, kaya-gaya, ka
krr, krarak, krarak
krie, krie, krie

drink cold water
feed on stones and bones
keep cool and fit

far out on your own

engaged
in long-distance communication

why does crow crow?
where does crow go?
what does crow know?

ask hawk
hovering up there in silence

ask the snowy owl

ask the great skua
and the rosy gull

all birds
talk dawn-talk
in different lingos.

Mountain Study*

1.
Why does one study?

for the white-gathered element –
having shaken the letters
to become unlettered

living
in the unlettered light.

2.
Every now and then
I go up into the mountains:
fire and snow –
trudging for hours
along the black line of the river
following it right to the crest
or, when the snow's gone
moving up through the forest
to the thin grass and the rocks
the high country –
up there in the stillness
thinking of nothing
only the body moving.

3.
Extraordinary ontological territory.

4.
Or in my study
with the books of calligraphy
drinking tea or white wine and slowly

leafing through the pages:
Song of the Diaphanous Mirror
Thousand Character Essay
Account of the Retreat of Quietude
The Pavilion of the Drunken Old Man
Treatise on Understanding...

5.
But the finest piece of calligraphy
I've ever set eyes on
(back a few years on Taiwan)
is a letter of thirty characters
written by Wang Hsi-chih
in a tough winter of the 4th century
to a good friend of his
asking him how he was faring
in these cold days
a piece of calligraphy which
under the title of
'Clear Sky Just Before Snow'
changed hands for a thousand years
each of its possessors
renaming his study in its honour
so that for a thousand years
somewhere in China
there was a 'Just Before Snow' study.

6.
If I named this study of mine
after the pair of scrolls
hanging there on the wall:

seven
mile

stream
shine
bright
outside

ten
thousand
hills
autumn
view

it would have to be something like
The Study of the Seven Mile Stream
or
The Study of the Ten Thousand Hills.

7.
In the Study of the Ten Thousand Hills
reading:
'Those who know truth
are not the equals
of those who love it
and those who love it
are not the equals of those
who take active delight in it'.

8.
Also writing:
all morning
this quiet thing happening
taking shape, unshaping, reshaping
between me, the language
and the snow
trying adjectives, so many adjectives

running through verbs
(a fine flurry of verbs)
what name for it all, now
midday, and
so little left, only
cool – stillness – soft
drifting – glow...
when, opening a Chinese grammar
(red binding still holding
the smell of Glasgow)
my eyes fall on *ta yü hsüeh*:
great rain snow.

9.
Movements in the snowy silence
what that line is
and this
no concern now with sense
only a calligraphy
a nameless and meaningless writing
to say without saying
the flurried fullness of
the inner murmuring of
the snowy silence.

Hölderlin in Bordeaux*

Not overgiven to conversation
when opinions
began trotting off the tongues
he tended to go away
for a walk along the river

'Why be a poet in such wretched times? ...
I do what I can as well as I can...
it all belongs
to the work in hand...'

That was in the red days of Autumn
with the grapes ripened
on the Garonne hills
and the memories of friends
who had left on ship
from the windy promontory...

Back in Germany
they had nothing for him
but he would go back
back
back to what?
some window overlooking a forest maybe
a little philosophical light...

Every day boats left the harbour
for the Indies, the Americas
he paced the quays
and watched them leaving
his journey
lying in another direction –
but how far would he be able to go

when everything was overgrown
with habit and with triviality
and mere opinion?

One may think of Greece
translate the tragedies
indulge in that archaic hyperbole
dream the ideal
the landscape had changed
utterly changed
he'd felt it crossing Auvergne
that awful night
losing his way
in the ice and snow
he'd felt it
the landscape had changed
colder
craggier
more massive –
poetry itself would have to change

No gods to sing to
in a sun-filled theatre
a nothingness to face
in an open expanse...

Walking the streets of Bordeaux
in the red days of September
watching how the shadows
moved slowly with the sun
seeing at some high window
a beautiful face
that was there, then gone

He would have to learn
how to travel alone.

Reading Han Shan in the Pyrenees*

1.
The disciples of Buddha
called him 'poet-monk'
those of Lao-Tzu called him
'hermit and mystic'
and the Confucianists said he was
a crazy eccentric
who sometimes talked sense

for himself
he was just Cold Mountain
doing his best
never knowing exactly
where it was leading him.

2.
Du Guangting (850–933)
in his *Shanxian Shiyi*
says Han Shan
'lived on Mt Cuiping
in the Tiantai Mts'

for the Taoists
the Tiantai range
was one of those places
'where men grow wings'

every now and then
he'd go down to the Guoqing monastery
to get food from the kitchen
but mostly he was up there
among the white clouds.

3.
Hadn't always been there though
talks of Red Sparrow Street
in Chang'an
where he must have raised the dust
(memories of sweet little girls:
'young girls playing in the twilight
the breeze blows their perfume over the roads')
before making for the heights.

4.
An unorthodox character
outside the classifications
he'd do a little zazen when it suited him
but made fun of the 'straight backs'
and 'shaven pates' in general

tao-buddhist, okay
but let's just say
mountain-poet
and get into the poems

all three hundred and eleven of them.

5.
'A certain smart alec by the name of Wang
said my poems were all wrong
and that I had no sense of prosody
they make me laugh with their "correct" poetry
it's just blind men singing about the sun'

let me find a few men with clear eyes
said Han Shan
and my poems will go round the world.

6.
'I sauntered off to see a great monk
misty mountains, mile after mile
the old fellow showed me the way back home:
the round lamp of the moon'

'strolling about on Huading Hill
sky clear, marvellous day'

'when the moon's bright
and all white
you can forget about East and West'.

7.
Those Cold Mountain poems
are like a day with two dawns.

Eleven Views of the Pyrenees

1.
They come to this studio
to discuss reality

all I ever say is
look out there at the mountain.

2.
On those fifteen snowy peaks
nothing moves
except, very slowly, the clouds.

3.
Gusty squalls of rain

and then
a white light, trembling
on a rock without a name.

4.
No birds

only a distant whispering –
the wind?

5.
A thin blue line
in the morning mist

that too is the mountain.

6.
Body absolutely still

the mountain
and a barking dog.

7.
Ah, Pyrenees
Pyrenees, ah
ah, Pyrenees.

8.
In the silence I've come to know
even the word 'emptiness' is all too loud,

9.
Three thousand books

in order to say
one single mountain.

10.
Today
on this blue afternoon

the mountain is *breathing*.

11.
The most limpid air

an unheard wind
that blows on the heights.

In the Sea and Pine Country*

1.
Meditation isn't mummification
it's quick movement
that enlightens the mind
those waves
crossing and intercrossing
rising and breaking
here in this dawn
that
is the perfect *zazen*.

2.
Here
on the white beach
with nothing in my rucksack
but an empty notebook:
'OK, we know you've studied
but what have you SEEN?'
– Shoji to Hakuin –
waiting and watching.

3.
Thinking of another shore
– no, not *the* Other Shore –
I keep going back
to that local shore
a thousand miles away
and what I see there
is nothing marvellous or pure
I see myself pitching
a basin of wormy old meat

from the butcher's shop
into the tide
and the gulls swooping down
in a fierce ragged
wing-flapping flurry
for the feed.

4.
Slap slap of the tide
I must be about eight years old
sitting on a rock
it's raining
a grey wet world
watching the tide come in
swirling round the rock...

5.
There are no rocks here
only long miles
of absolute sand
with pools that mirror
the summer sky
a flock of gulls
over yonder
flutters into movement now and then
and an occasional cry
enlarges the silence.

6.
Long silence, long joyance.

7.
At midday
I go into the woods
from the shining sands
to the dark bed of pine:
whin-bushes yellow
crimson gashes on the tree-trunks
sharp smell of resin.

8.
'Learn of the pine
from the pine'.

9.
Quiet
the wind has dropped
now it is a question
of looking and smelling:
crimson gash, yellow flower
take them
and set the mind on fire.

10.
Let the light come
so you can say
really seeing them:
crimson gash, yellow flower
(seeing and saying
then
is power).

11.
Change of scene:
dark sea
the red circle of the sun.

12.
Tonight I shall sleep in the woods.

The Residence of Solitude and Light*

1.
Suddenly I *see* my table
this table I've worked at
for the past nine years
with the copper lamp
the papers under stones
the bamboo vase of pens and pencils
on the wall beside it
a page of Chinese seals
and the photo of a naked *yakshi*
at the Eastern gate of Sanchi.

2.
For nine years my horizon
has been these blue ridges:
this morning snow-scattered
early October –
'autumn hills
here and there
smoke rising'
(Blyth quotes Gyôdai
and refers to Turner).

3.
Books come in through the post:
Studien zur Geschichte Osteuropas
The Buddhist Sogdian Texts
Alphabetisches Verzeichnis zum Kao Seng Ch'uan
Essays on T'ang Society
Gupta Temple Architecture
Études Song

The Magic Oracles of Japan
Cahiers du Pacifique
Die Inseln des Stillen Ozeans
Discourses on the Vigyana Bhairava Tantra
Contributions to the Anthropology of Nepal...

4.
Working and reworking
the same texts
over and over again
losing all sense
of 'production' and 'publication'
and 'furthering one's reputation'
engaged rather in something
outside literature
that might rightly be called
poetic yoga.

5.
Fascinated by Valéry's analytical geometry of the mind
by Chao's discovery of Buddhism
by the grammars of Khalil and Panini
the drawings of Sesshu
the yoga of Patanjali:
a notion of psychophysical economy
making clean gestures
in clarified space.

6.
Like Valéry
saying over and over to myself
beata solitudo
sola beatitudo

but enjoying also
unlike that purest of pure intellectuals
(though he too had his 'long regard')
enjoying almost mindlessly
the solar field
out there this October morning:
golden sun diffused through mist

7.
Thinking
of Khalil's definition of reality:
$A + A - A - A + A - A + A...$
maybe that's what I've been working at
these last nine years
the result being:

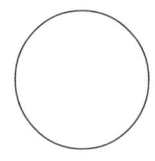

◯

– a pleasant sensation of nothingness-potential
a breathing space
the beautiful breast of emptiness.

BOOK VI

Handbook for the Diamond Country*

Trans-world express. Here the mass is reduced to fragments and the long movement is broken down into moments. But every fragment contains the whole. And a moment can carry a great space of time, shot through, shall we say, with the whiteness of eternity.

Another Little Autobiography

I've been in and out of institutions
banged a few doors

in and out of lives and loves
come away with a few scars

I've gone deeper into poetry
the space where the mind clears –

now I walk in my own image
follow me who dares.

Culture Telegrams

1. *Yesterday*
Move over, Plato
a problematic culture
the age of anxiety.

2. *Today*
Moving to and fro
a questing culture
the age of emptiness-joyance.

Drinking Green Tea in the Rue St Antoine

Smells good and faraway present
tea from the island
of Taiwan
three in the afternoon
soft rain falling
on St Antoine –
earth oils, mountain stillness.

Archaic Territory*

It was a white space on the map

Fa-hsien came by there
on his way to India
likewise Hsûan-tsang

'the sky opens, a peak reveals itself
as though risen from emptiness, a monastery appears'

came Dutreil de Rhins, came Frédéric Grenard
finding terracotta figurines, fragments of pottery
and an Indian manuscript among the oldest we possess:

a version of the *Dhammapada* written on birchbark.

The Absolute Body

The absolute body wakens
puts on pants and shirt

and goes out into the streets.

A Fragment of Yellow Silk

Among all that display
of ancient treasure
one thing remains in my mind

a fragment of yellow silk

hardly bigger
than a breast or a hand

unearthed on the road
from Ch'ang-an to Antioch
via Samarkand.

> (Exhibition, recent Chinese archaeological discoveries,
> Paris)

Intellectual Gathering

I've read much Hindu literature
over the past few years
close on a hundred well-studied books
but when I stood there with the girl
in the darkblue sari
and might have been expected
in that intellectual gathering
to make some appropriate conversation
all I could think of
was the darkblue sari
and her nakedness under it.

Gujarati

For years a girl like you
had walked through my mind
but in the sordid precincts
of the Gorbals, Glasgow –
you carried an ancient
Gujarat with you

When you combed your hair
I saw an art come alive
when you unclothed yourself
it was stone become flesh
and when you opened your thighs
I penetrated India.

Knowledge Girl

>'Yellow body I adore'
>(folksong, Laos)

Now the great space
is all around me
and you golden flower
within me

the Eastern art I made my study
is your flesh your bones
the curve of your eye
your tongue and its tones

in the presence
of your naked breasts
religion has no reality

and the smooth beauty
of your loving belly
realizes philosophy.

Japanee

Métro Clignancourt

No longer howling city
no longer stations on the underground

the Japanee girl stands quiet there

like a blade of frosted grass
on a distant island.

Autumn Departure

> 'Red leaves on the stream'
> (Harumichi no Tsuraki)

Sunday morning
bright and chill
on the concourse at Orly

flight for Tokyo
via Tel Aviv
gate 50

one word to be spoken
now
for ever

if you want to know
my feelings
ask the East-flowing river.

Crossing the Beauce

All those little villages of the plains

Colvainville, Loinville
Oisème, Champseru, Umpeau

and then this other one:
Thoreau

no, nobody, not even at the Mairie
had ever heard of Henry...

we got back on the road
watching the land open wide
the sky full of ocean cloud.

The Cormorants

It's where the Seine
passes through the Normandy hills
by chalk-white bluffs

an early March morning
in the grey mist and the haar

there's an island there

nestled and huddled in its trees
a hundred cormorants
calling and staring

making sudden outgoings

then back to the branches
staring and calling.

At Honfleur

A high wind's blowing round the old salt-cellar
and the sea-brine impregnates the kirk's dark wood

'This is the logbook of *L'Aimable Rose*
that traded down the Guinea coast
in the last years of the Revolution'

at the quiet inn on Quarantine Quay
the talk this noon is of business with Peking

Baudelaire is still dreaming in the Cats' Hotel

the ghost of Champlain is wailing with the gulls

'Handmade fishing boats
many choise inside – please to enter'

blue slates gleaming in Atlantic weather.

(Normandy coast)

An Evening at Yvetot

So there I was in the Hôtel du Havre
Rue Guy de Maupassant, at Yvetot

that afternoon, out from Paris along the Seine
we'd crossed the rainswept plateau of Caux
watching a grey heron flapping in the grey
and streams full of soft green grasses silently rippling

at St Wandrille, the skull of the man
(a disciple they tell me of Columban)
listened to forty monks chanting gregorian

in the Hôtel du Havre, room 101
I lay listening to nothing but the rain.

The Burgundian Trip

Little sharpfaced hawks peering down
from telephone wires on the road to Avallon

a deer leaping out of the Morvan woods
glancing quickly at the traffic
and plunging back into the forest darkness

choughs chattering knowingly
around the chimneys of Clamecy

while dollar dialogues with yen
over Bâtard Montrachet and Savigny-lès-Beaune
the waters of the Brenne and the Armançon flow quietly on

rain blurs the towers of Semur and the tombs of Pouilly.

On the Plains

All around Poitiers
flat country
and the signs of a dry summer

grass burnt yellow
sunflowers black

the lusty troubadours
have gathered in the Sympatic Bar
where all the talk
is balls and divisions

now is the time to follow
the laconic track of the crow.

Message

Not far from a place called St-Quentin-les-Anges

a roadside rest-park

on the wooden table
somebody's scratched five letters

'world'.

South Roads, Summer

1.
Mid-afternoon:
blue light flickering
on the silent crags.

2.
Where did the wind go? –
dawn coming quietly
over the hills.

>   (Alpilles)

Winter Morning Train*

> 'Autonomous and emancipated, he travels hither and
> thither like a leaf in the wind of the *Samskara*'
> (Astâvakra gîtâ)

Between Béziers and Narbonne
vineyards under frost
and a big red sun
running mad on the horizon.

No Four-Star Hôtel*

Sardines and rice
rice and sardines

with a red tomato

rice and sardines
sardines and rice

with a red tomato.

                (Arles)

Café du Midi*

Lo cors a fresc, sotil e gai

Sitting here
in the shadow
with literature

I see Mireille
keen beauty
crossing the square

O night
please bring me
to her body bare.

Nameless

Which one of the writers
ever
caught the sense of

difficult beauty's
little tits

see where she walks
there
clothed in the wind

over the white sand.

Avignon

That July I was down in Avignon
lodged in a shady hotel
in the Rue des Trois Faucons

now recollecting that time
I'm thinking not at all
about the much advertised cultural festival

I'm seeing once again
(in the discreet little Requien museum)
an enormous lump of gypse crystal

and the carcass of a wolf, as though live
killed in the region of Notre-Dame-des-Neiges
in late November 1875.

Autumn at Meyrueis

Above all
the chalky desert of the Causse Méjean

Meyrueis nestling in its hollow
the smell of smoke and melon in the lanes
and in the Lozère bazaar
the last walking-sticks and *bouffadous* of the season

here in the forest
flitting in the golden sunlight
a fragile dragonfly.

In the Lozère

1.
A circle of white rocks
hawk hovering –
high noon on the Causse.

2.
Sunday morning
in the misty forest:
the screech of a jay.

The White Mistral

'The Mistral is "white" when it is not accompanied
by clouds and precipitation'
(Book of Navigation)

Beyond the turmoil
of living, loving and dying
all at once the sky clears

a white wind blowing.

Fragments of a Red Sea Journal

East of Suez
the land is red
marked by a maze
of dried watercourses
with blue mountain ridges
vapouring into infinity

...

In the country of the Somali
the earth is a tigerskin

...

Aden, Djibouti, Ogaden
the end of an old line

...

This is where the script of the continent
opens out on to the empty ocean.

Paradise Lodge[*]

Baie Lazare, Mahé, Indian Ocean

The sou-easter's come in early
wind crackling the palm fronds
the sea rising rough
sudden showers

I'm ensconced in these 'super de luxe' chambers
facing the expanse of the sanskrit sea

drinking southafrican champagne
'elegant dry'
Bellingham, est. 1693

on the wall there's a print by Audubon
but the framer's gone over the bird's name
no doubt thinking nobody anyway will give a damn

all I can say for the moment is
by the light of this flickering lamp
it's a great powerful rosy creature
fishing in a swamp.

Equatorial*

1.
Mid-May in the Indian Ocean
and a steady south-east monsoon blowing

albas skim by with a shrill wee cry
dark terns yammer far down the sky
saltheads craik in the burning blue
while the little ground dove goes *curroo-curroo.*

2.
Here's roughly what the filao said
as it waved and whispered above my head

growing into the immensity of the skies
I have no mind really to philosophize
let me just sway away all day
in this highly contemplative way.

3.
As twilight falls over land and sea
red bats will be flitting from tree to tree

night come, I'll lie out under the stars
the Great Way almost within foot reach
listening to the long tide tell the roll of the years
while ancient turtles trundle up the beach.

Turtle Trail

Under the full moon
out she comes

lumbering, levering
along the soft sand

scoops out a hole
finds it uncongenial

moves further up
and starts again

drops the clutch in
covers it over

then heaves her way back down
into the ocean

mission accomplished.

In a Bar at Victoria

'My mind is full of the old schooner days
all those dawns and sunrises'
said Lazare Lorient

'Me, it's lugging those big bags of cocos
down to the beach at Providence'
said Léon Malaquais

'I can't forget the first time I set foot
on the eery shore of Aldabra'
said Pierre Dequincey

'What a bunch of sentimental bums
all I remember's the last rum – or was it beer?'
said Blaise Lafleur.

(Mahé Island, Indian Ocean,
a summer evening)

The Insular Contemplations of Pascal Pandanus

He who had always gone around
with all hell and heaven imaged in his head
now sat
reduced almost to nothing
under a roof of corrugated iron
on an island in the Indian Ocean

listening to the trees

the slow heavy takamaka
the flustering palms that hiss with a noise like rain
the filao full of silent grace

saying in the course of his contemplation:
'once you really hear and see
you have no more need of imagination'

a great tortoise, antediluvian
lumbering up the pathway to the house
seemed to give weight
to this iconoclastic affirmation

in the evening
he'd go down to the bay
watching, say
yellow-flippered hawksbill turtles
parrotfish, angelfish, wrasses
the dark nurse-shark
a spotted ray...

so it went on
in a long low monotone
day after timeless day.

Philosopher on the Beach

The baroque philosopher
walks the balmy beach

talking to himself
like some phenomenal lizard

observes a crested tern
and thinks: Schopenhauer...

espies a bird of paradise
and cries: Nietzsche!

measures his brain-waves
all the long afternoon

mixes metaphysics with his gin
when the sun goes down

when the existential sun
goes down.

The Island without a Name

The sounding of the silence here
is a *kerrak-rrok-rrok*
pronounced by dark birds

the endless emptiness of the sky
is filled with slowmoving cloud
from the open ocean

meditation is and is not the name for what goes on

a single, sun-bright concentration
while a thousand blue waves break on the horizon.

Being, Nothingness and a Bottle of Rum

These are the windless times
the doldrums

rockabye baby
(sung by a drunken sailorboy)

in the treetops
the noddies don't even nod

on the ground
the tortoises work to a schedule
Dead Slow and Stop

here in the cabin
I hesitate, sweating
between a treatise on tropical nihilism
and total inarticulate nirvana.

On the African Banks

West of Mahé
in the Outer Isles
part of the Amirantes archipelago

the African Banks

a dot on the ocean
a speck in the cosmos

it was here
Zebediah MacLaren
off the schooner *Fantasia*

first came across
with trembling jubilation

a band of Rosy Terns.

The Afternoon of the Phaetons

They kept coming and coming
a pair of them
in under the filao tree

searching for a place to stay?

any time I'd seen those tropic birds before
they were high in the air
looking as though they knew exactly
where they were heading for

but here they were questing for something

they went round and round and round
exotically fluttering question marks
like a philosophy in the making

all afternoon I watched them
no nearer to any particular line of thought
but full of that sense of general white-flying
and the fascination of a newly discovered place.

(Indian Ocean)

Sunrise

At the hour of the rising sun

great grey herons
sentinelled here and there
on the shore of the lagoon

while a hundredfold squadron of frigates
sway slowmotionly
high up in the wind zone.

North Station Note

Standing at a window
in the Hotel Terminus Nord
a dreary night in November

down there in the street
the bars are packed:

the *Villes du Nord*
the *Rendez-vous des Belges*
the *Quai de l'Espérance*

'Départ – Departing – Abfahrt'

Boulogne, Calais, St Omer
Oostende, Brussels, Copenhagen

it's an old song with a haunting refrain:
cold sirens singing in the rain.

At the Red Cloister

'Under this earth lies
Hugo van der Goes
painter and brother
who lived out all his days
here at the Red Cloister'

at the chill end of October
five centuries later
I walk along the pathways
among the reddening trees
and the quiet, green, fish-laden pools

listening to the crows.

                                                (Brussels)

A Raw Blue Morning in Antwerp*

For Eloi the Slater

The rumbling of lorries
along innumerable quays

Bataviastraat, Montevideostraat

the sun's an eternally
uncut diamond

while the *Nove Anna* from Copenhagen
unloads tomato juice

Maria José counts her cash
in the Caribbean Bar.

The House of Erasmus

At Anderlecht, in this uncertain Autumn

behind the redbrick walls
lie the cluttered books and letters of the Rotterdamer
heard by all Europe
in that rhetorical time

but out here this cold afternoon
in the frost-bitten garden
there's a rose, only a rose of the last days
white, with a silent, distant perfume.

Letter from Amsterdam

It's raining
it's been eight weeks long dark raining
and I've been sitting in this empty room
listening to the rain
it's a Europe of rain
(all the bullshit of Europe
washed away in the rain)
and if I speak of Europe
it's because I'm thinking of India
looking at a photograph
cut from a newspaper
pinned to my wall:
the photo of a woman
an Indian woman
a pariah woman
her dark (very dark) face
lit by a smile
a very naked smile –
the WHITE LAUGHTER of Shiva.

The Tower at Tübingen

A wildered garden, a bit of a boat
and the Neckar flowing slowly by

every moment a symbol of eternity

the seasons, rhythmically, came and went
rain, snow, so many shades of blue
(his intelligence still wondered what it meant)
the sun shone, leaves fell, the cold winds blew

three large windows, a familiar land
the river, the path, the sky, the wood
a gradual emptying of his mind
an increasing sensation that all was good

all was good, at the final edge
and a light gleamed on the far horizon

a gentle breeze lingering among the sedge
below the 'Hölderlin Tower', at Tübingen.

Schopenhauer in Berlin

The talk was live that noontime at the inn
Plato dancing in the air with Kant –
but he broke it all up suddenly with this:
'Did you see the look on that dog's face?'

and made his way over to the edge of town
outside the world of push and illusion
for his daily walk among primary things

'Doctor of Philosophy, from Dantzig'
was still how he styled himself
saying polite hallos to passers-by
his mind, like a Buddha's, intent on nothingness:
cold rain falling on yellow grass.

Kant in Königsberg

This city, old and grey

where every day
I take out my books
moving through the paragraphs
travelling in a difficult way
out into clarity

'Enlightenment is the exit
from humanity's self-inflicted
lack of adequate language'

the daily chore, the daily routine

one of these mornings
I promise myself
I'll take a long quiet walk
along the Baltic coast
up beyond Fischhausen.

Stockholm

I was sitting in *Rydbergs*
outside it was Stockholm
and it was snowing...

all along the pavements
little flames flickered a wintry welcome

at Skansen
amid scenes of old Sweden
(while a wolverine
prowled among the rocks)
there was singing and circle-dancing

over the bay
in from the archipelago
white boats loomed out of the mist

but there in *Rydbergs* restaurant
at two in the afternoon
it was only the snow
the gently falling
dreamily falling snow –
and the ghost of Strindberg
staggering past the window.

In the Blue Tower

The best times were at Dalarö
out there in the archipelago

trying to create
the way nature creates
among wind, wave and rock

then came the hate
volcanic and vicious
and the crazy ideas I threw out
(remember the rue d'Assas in Paris?)
with the laugh of a maniac

looking around here now:
the battered old kirk-book
the shady lamp with the crimson eye
all those dingy, dungeon ledgers…

tomorrow, over in the Deer-Park
I'll photograph the clouds.

>   (The Strindberg House, Drottninggatan 85
>   Stockholm)

Strindberg at Lund

Here in Lund
I live more and more alone
joy only in my work

long indeed it is
the road to Damascus...

what a hellish mess
has been this life of mine

back of it all
that longing
for purity and beauty

April on the skerry.

A Consideration of the Norwegian Sea

Take a strong first throw
say from Bergen up the coast to Tromsø

here the cystalline waters of Greenland
meet sultry salt floods out from Mexico

making for mixings, eddyings, vortices

codfish
spawn in the frontal zone

knowing birds travel the wide winds

pack-ice drifts
with current and tide

from rock to jagged rock
lighthouses send out signs –

I lie in this bare room
following out the lines.

                                        (Storgata, Tromsø)

At the Head of the Fjord

Pale blue passages
(the paths along which
incipient Spring is travelling)
open in the ice

snow gives way to sand

little streams trickle from the rocks
into widening water

all the way down the shore
straggly clumps
of silvery, stunted
red-tinted birches

inch by inch
(with quiet insistence
and with subtle authority)
the lyrical influences
advance.

Letters from the Lofoten

1.

Moving up the Raftsund
in a silence almost total
broken only by the *swish* of the prow
slicing the flatblackwaters

skimming low over the bow
an eagle gives us a startled glance
before beating up to the cloudy heights
on the starboard side.

2.

Arctic light, archaic rock
dark masses looming out of ghostly whitenesses
the earth-book of the Lofoten islands
is one stark ice-page after another

on rough grass by the shore's edge
you come across a codhead skeleton
left there by some gull's picking
gub agape in a soundless shriek.

3.

Lief 1-10-1883, Haakon 8-5-1910
the stones in this improvised graveyard
bear only those bare forenames
belonging to men with no folks to speak of

the almost perfectly anonymous ones
hands hard, lips numb, eyes cold
migrants of the northern sea-roads
seasonal fishers in the fjords of the West.

Bergen–Oslo Express

Thin mist moving over snaefell heights
waterfalls cascading into chasms
ice-blocks strewn along chill riverbanks

acres of grey rock chaos

outside Myrdal we get involved in a little blizzard
hefty snow driving wild
across straight pine and twisted birch

gradually the driving turns into a drifting...

'Allo, allo, the next station is Ustaoset
here the left side is the one to use'

my neighbour, a gentle good-looker with golden hair
snores gently, like some ancient muse

farther down the car
a starry-eyed, gimlet-spectacled skier
is engrossed in a New Testament

looking out hour after hour
at the passing landscape
I am, all in all, content.

Warsaw

Clip-clopping on the cobbles
an unseen horse

sweeping over the Vistula
driving dead leaves
across the thoroughfares
a chill wind heavy with rain

drinking white vodka
in this dark room
going through the images
of a time-worn album:
'*On the Eastern Frontier –
memory of the journey to Ukraine.*'

On the Baltic Coast

'Go to Hel'
said my friend
so I went

a long train journey
across the plains of Poland –
lake, pine, birch, moor

up to Dantzig

then a boat
almost empty of passengers
this late November
over here to the peninsula

now in this fishing village

combing the cold sands
for scattered amber

watching thin snow
falling on the Baltic Sea.

Black Sea Letter*

Recalling Ovid

Another Sarmatian winter setting in
goats blethering in what passes for a garden
rain falling when it isn't poisoned arrows
(how many summers since I smelled a Roman rose!)
eyes bleary, frosty weather on my chin

why bother writing yet another book?
well, it keeps my mind off stupid folk
the scratching of my stilus on the page
is music to my ears and cools my rage
I know now I'll be here until I croak

so, here's a man will listen to the snow
and let the hours come, long and slow
such distance and such silence, all I wish
salt fish is now my favorite dish
I was a famous Roman poet, years ago.

October on Corsica

It was the month of burnt leaves
and migratory birds

I was sitting in a café
on the waterfront at Calvi

the *Colombo* sightsee-er
(some would like to think
Cristoforo was born here)
lay moored for the season

but it was an Indian summer
in the bright October sun

as I drank my coffee slowly
(behind me a welter of history)
I watched with quiet pleasure
the blue waves beautifully performing
their cosmochaotic calligraphy.

Seneca's Exile

There are capes and capes
(I've known quite a few)
this one was the farthest

I was in exile
(that happens to the best)
because I had seduced
(that was the word they used)
the emperor's niece

greywhite rock
the perfume of wild thyme
wandering goats –
not neglecting the cheeses and oysters of Aleria
where you could still hear Greek

there I wrote book after book

I who had been trained
in philosophy and rhetoric
felt drawn now to geology
and, strangely, to meteorology

I speculated on clouds
I meditated at the edge of the sea
I read sermons in stones

a lot of those poems
(was it a mystic kind of gesture or plain despair?)
I buried under the heather
beside an old watch-tower
where no doubt they still are

later I wrote a skit on the emperor:
Claudius the Pumpkin

(burlesque literature
was about all that Rome could take any more)
describing his arrival in heaven
and his divine pumpkinification

later again
I was tutor to a murderous nitwit
the *duce*, Nero
but that's a part of history I choose to forget

for a while I toed the line
then finally I committed suicide
at the age of sixty-nine.

A Winter Evening in Bastia

The *Corsica Victoria*
festooned for Christmas
fills the new harbour with its bulk

over in the old port
(Arab voices
on the Quai du 1er Bataillon-de-choc)
at the cabin window
of a battered, baroque hulk
the skipper enjoys a crepuscular smoke

in the church of the holy saint Roch
(who wore the obscure pilgrim's cloak)
only a wandering cat
and a candle guttering in the dark.

Along the Adriatic

It was April
when we came along that coast

like travelling through a smoky mirror

salt, sand, long reeds
a white heron flying over the flats

and the sea's pale glitter.

Vico at Vatolla

These forest solitudes were exactly what I needed

here for nine years
I who was to be
the most adamant deserter from the literary ranks
and a prototype of the existential desperado
followed my own way
and wrote in my own wild tongue
(a mixture of Latin and Neapolitan lingo)
as far away from dusty scholastics
as from the techno-crazy moderns

I composed an autobiography
I invented a new philosophy

while my books go round the changing world
I, the other I, continue haunting
this leafy pathway though the ancient woods.

San Pelagio in the Rain

It was raining hard
when we got to San Pelagio

the big trucks on the fast road
spouted waterfalls from their wheels

a grey pall dark as lead
was lying over the Euganean hills

passing by, someone had said
there Messer Francesco Petrarca
first opened his honeyed mouth

I registered the fact but, raising my eyes
watched a band of honking geese
flying eagerly toward the South.

Found on the Shore

Ovid talking

I remember the rain at Brindisi that November
(Virgil there twenty years before
shaking with malaria
and so sick with humanity
he'd have burnt his most ambitious book)
it whispered round the inn
where we drank the last wine
and drummed, hummed and drummed
on the roof of the cabin:
Brindisi
with its homely fishing smacks
clustered in the harbour
and the long white beaches
of the Calabrian coast...
I at that time a broken man
taking a last whiff of Italy
(the fishy quays
the olives and the cypresses)
before moving out by the narrow channel
into a grey Adriatic
that smelt only of salt
and a wind of exile
whipping the sails –
but look out there in the waves
Proteus, the pharaoh of the seals!

The Last Days of the Academy

By the Christian's order
the doors were closed

so they went into exile
the last seven

Damascius the Syrian
Simplicius the Cilician
Eulamius the Phrygian
Priscianus the Lydian
Hermes and Diogenes, Phoenicians
and Isidorus, who was from Gaza

they went first to Persia
then dispersed
each one, alone

walking into the emptiness.

                                          (Athens, 6th century A.D.)

Xenophanes of Kolophon*

Poet and philosopher.
When the Persians invaded Asia Minor
he moved to Sicily

walking along the shore of that island
he wrote:

even if you stumble
on some rocks of the truth
you'll never know it all

he spoke of sea, wind, earth
clouds and rivers
and said that god was round.

Five Little Greek Ones

1.
Standing at the *stasis*
waiting for the metaphor:
night ride Delfi-Athina.

2.
A winter's day
on the white acropolis:
tap-tap, tap-tap-tap of the hammer.

3.
All that afternoon
coming back again and again
to the thoughtful-faced Kore.

4.
Under the national flag
listening (*kataresi, kataresi*)
to the pelagian wind.

5.
Up on the heights –
lights coming on all along the bay:
nightfall in Thessaloniki.

Patmos

Alexis signed the bull
Christopoulos the monk took it over

an island of thorn and heather
of no political interest whatsoever

books gathered there over the years
ranging from Saint John's delirium
to a life of the super-cool Buddha.

Europe in the Fall

After stravaiging round the Black Sea
with a little Stambuli
I came back into Europe via Athens

rain on the olive trees
and not a living soul on the Acropolis

(where has everybody gone
where the hell have they gone –
all gone down into the plain)

I sit in an empty café
drinking Turkish coffee

looking out on the rain.

Atlas

Myth can still hit you
momentarily in a Boeing

like the other morning, in mid-March
on the RAM to Morocco
along a great line of craggy nevadas

the ground country, green with a blue haze
then a contorted yellowred

with Tangiers
(from Tinga, wife of Anteas
who was son of Poseidon, the sea
and of Gaia, the earth)
looming up on the horizon

and farther down the coastline
the glistening white world of Casablanca.

Bedouin

They'd come up from the Tendrara country
because of the drought and no grass

then the rented truck had broken down

so they'd pitched their tents there
in that area of wind and scrub

'Is there anything you need?' –
it was an old woman, small and spare
blue tatooings on a wizened face
hands and feet caked in dust
who'd hirpled over to speak with us

'Thank you, no, we're just moving around
from place to place in the Oriental
stopping here and there to look at the land'

'It is good to walk and look
while you're on earth, see the world
under the earth, you see nothing'

rosy light on darkblue rock
white snailshells dotting hard parched soil
a black-winged hawk

'May Allah keep you and open the way, amen.'

(Morocco, the Oriental region)

A Morning's Work

The old black man
in tattered shirt and faded blue shorts
walks up and down the beach
up and down the beach
slowly
all morning
on the lookout –
then suddenly he crouches
eyes fixed
and stalks into the sea
his net at the ready
casts it
and carefully
hauls it in:

ten silver fish
flapping in its meshes.

(near Gabès, Tunisia)

South-West Corner News

'Empty activity'

Blue misty morning
sun white thistle
can't see the mountains
but there's snow on the peaks
fell last week night
will be gleaming noon

'Egyptian tanks
crossing Suez Canal
Israeli reservists
rushing to battle'

red autumn here
in south-west corner
Pyrenean silence
privileged? absolute?

drinking tea in rice-grain bowl

somewhere somebody
has to reach the cool.

(Atlantic Pyrenees)

The Pinelands

At Sabres
of an April evening:
pine logs burning in the grate
and a chill rain falling

at Sabres
of an April morning:
the cry of a pheasant
in the forest stillness.

Port-de-Richard

'The government killed us', he said

he was an old man
with a much-worn seaman's cap rammed on his skull
and it was a once neat harbour
on the banks of the Gironde

'they killed us off
when they set up that petroleum place
over to Bordeaux'

in the old days (only ten years ago)
they fished, a bunch of them, for sturgeon and eels –
now all the fish are cancered
you can see their backbones through the wasted flesh

'the bed of the estuary was packed with oysters
you could pick them up as easy as mushrooms'

now they've been raked away by dredgers
with only a few shells still nailed as reminders
above the lintels of the wooden shacks

as the old man talked about the days
when he'd be out there away in the open
('I took in my sails when the swallows passed
and when the swallows came back I was off again')
where the yellow waters mingle with the blue
I looked at the stone quays infested with weeds
hearing the sea wind sighing among the reeds.

A Golden Day on the Gulf

Out of Socoa in a red dawn
aboard the *Apocalypse*
(used to sail from St-Jean-de-Luz)
Cpt Santiago Michelena
with a rough crew of Basques and Portuguese

boa viagem! boa pesca!

midday saw us way out away
in the Bay of Biscay
which is here the Gulf of Gascony
amid a roaring confusion

ah!
the thousand daughters of the ocean.

Equinox

Those tidal days

when the thunder
talks through the rain

and a lightning beauty
flashes over the brain.

Monte Perdido

Walking long hours
along the dark Ordessa

'Buenas!', 'Hola!'

up to the grey mass
streaked with snow
of Monte Perdido.

Extraordinary Moment

I have been working all morning
from midnight till eleven o'clock

now I sit drinking the wine of Maury
watching the first snow on the mountains

I can describe neither the redness of the wine
nor the whiteness of the mountains.

Mountain Study in Winter

1.
Like the Room of Purity and Freshness
in the Tennô Palace at Kyoto

cool working here all day
with an occasional bowl of tea or soup

clean hard line of the mountains
to keep verse and thought high and in order.

2.
Rustling wind among the birches
the silver sun blazing a fir

I've opened one book after another
all along this winter

now I'm just sitting in the emptiness
enjoying the sun-filled stillness.

Rock Crystal

There are ninety ways up the Pic d'Ossau.

'It smells of winter,' he said – a shepherd with a couple of hundred sheep to look after. Asked what day it was, saying that if you stayed too long up there (he's been up three months), you begin to have 'a goat's head'.

In the refuge at six thousand feet, reading: some time after his death in China, Bodhidharma was seen in the Ts'ong-ling mountains, *walking back to India with one shoe in his hand...*

Mist came down in the afternoon, just little patches at first, lit by the sun, then gradually accumulating, till it was one great silent drifting mass. As you walked, your shadow was projected on the mist, hugely, and with an aura.

Met a mineralogist who told me of a big lump of crystal he'd found embedded in the rock at an almost unreachable place. Said he'd have to break it into fragments before he could bring it down.

In a Mountain Hut

Suddenly the thunder
made itself heard

then in the stillness
came the far song

of one single bird.

Prose for the Col de Marie-Blanque

Winter deep in the mountains. Thick falling snow. Here at the Col de Marie-Blanque, we're walking, slowly.

'No study, no book learning, you just let it filter through the mind.'

There's nothing at all impressive about the Col de Marie-Blanque. Just a little mountain pass. No place for sensational exploits. Something else.

'A reality man has the diamond of knowledge.'

The path moves up through the wood: pine, oak, birch. There's nothing much to be said. We don't talk. We just put one foot in front of the other, and let the snow do the work.

'Only wolves live in the dark silent wood.'

We're the white wolves of those final spaces. We love this distance, this winter light. Our life is secret. It's no longer ours.

'If the great frost has never bitten the branches, how can plum blossom be fragrant?'

When they ask me what religion I belong to, I'll say: the religion of the Col de Marie-Blanque.

Saturday Night Whisky Talk*

'Ueno? Asakusa?'

Eight o'clock tolling
on the Bizanos church bell

I'm thinking of a haiku by Bashô

and of a lady I did know
long long ago
in Tokyo.

The Winter-Spring Phase

Eight days ago
up at the Col de Marie-Blanque
it was a frozen world
with snow drifting
over arctic conifers

this morning
from this quiet room
I look at the mountain
in the warm white
misty light
of early Spring.

The Road of Light

1.
Port of Bayonne:
a boat loading Spanish quartz
bound for Bergen.

2.
Dark, dark
a sudden flash of sunlight
illuminates the yellow whin.

                            (A wild walk in the Basque country)

Wakan*

This is beautiful, this is beautiful
nothing is more beautiful than this

blue light breaking in the mountains
moon going down through the rain

nothing is more beautiful than this.

Misty Mornings in the South-West Studio

1.
Cold mist
red leaves, yellow leaves
a dog barking.

2.
Village of smoke
hills wrapped in mist
mountain whiteness.

3.
Young mountain peak
take off that shirt of mist
so I can see your snowy nakedness.

A Little Epistle from Spain

A day in the depths of Northern Spain
on hill paths
listening to the falling rain

left the pleasant town of Pau
crossed a plateau of the Pyrenees
scattered with the lingering remains of winter snow

now in this village tavern:
bullfight posters
jugs of red wine, loud music from Madrid
but also

the sense of thin dark silent trails
up through the history of Europe.

Extremadura

In this late, very late September

over the Sierra de Guadalupe, thick cloud
heavy rain sweeping olive and whin
farther to the West, a broken frontier
bright with ocean blues

these were the gateways to the Americas

(when the slaughter was done
they'd strike a sword in the ground
Orellano, Pizarro and the rest
and declare to the four quarters
on the lines they'd laid down
the foundation of a town)

a few miles on, at Trujillo
where Our Lady of the Victories
turning her back on the congregation
looks out over the rocks
and where the stones of the old castle
have been handed back over to the crows

a chill clear wind was rising.

Passage West

In search of red America
fisher of origins

'to begin to begin again'

now up in the high North-west

smoky whiteness in the air
soul of winter
breaking out into blue yelling star

the blood leaps
the hand touches roots

the centre starts from everywhere

reality's blazed.

The American Pelican

With his long, long shanks
and longish nose
looks a bit like a Yankee
in fact, strangely like Mister Henry Thoreau

an archaic bird
lived and revelled in the warm waters of the world
about thirty million years ago

went almost extinct
thanks to DDT

but looks now as if
he'll still be around
(two beats and a glide, two beats and a glide)
when *homo* so-called *sapiens*
has played his last hand.

Old Man in Dogtown

In memoriam Charles Olson

'A teeny weeny one
for the road,' he said
and went out again
into the grey wind

white clapboard houses
fish bones, weather vanes
salty memories
this place, another space

old man in baggy pants
bald, gasping, lumbering
still pressing forward
with an eye to the open.

Somewhere in New England

East-west afternoon:
leaves of grass
reflected in my bowl of tea.

While Reading Robert Frost

A running shadow
brought my eye up off the page
and there outside
enveloped in the mist
I saw a hunched-up rabbit
munching sage.

Letter to Alaska

This is for the Arctic Loon
the Red-necked Grebe
and the Pelagic Cormorant

for the Red-legged Kittiwake
the Grey-tailed Tattler
and the Canada Goose

for the Northern Fulmar
the Great Blue Heron
and the Tundra Swan

may they escape the black flood
may they find their way into the open.

A Snowy Morning in Montreal

Some poems have no title
this title has no poem

it's all out there.

At Cape Tumult

Like one of those days
at the melting of the ice
so many thousand years ago

earth bruised, rock scarred
(the beginnings there of what writing?)
but the cold gone, and the anguish

even in the shattering of the waves
a great serenity.

                                        (Mouth of the St Lawrence)

Tadoussac

Off this point
you can see whales blowing

big whales from Greenland
breasting the St Lawrence

you're no longer in Canada, friend
you're up in the white wastes
of Melville's mind
there's metaphysics in the wind!

West Labrador

Cold sun on the taïga
at times a faint rainbow
thick moss on the forest floor
rivers, lakes, rapids

ice on the Schefferville dirt roads
thin snow on the forest ground
Indians out prowling with 30-30s
on the hunt for caribou
hare or white partridge.

Achawakamik

Up on the edge of Hudson's Bay
between the River Severn and the River Winisk
there is a place called Achawakamik

in the Cree language, that means
'a place to watch from'

they say, on the point of dying, an old man
planted his wigwam there
so that in his dying he might see
the forests and the waters
and the breath of the great spirit

if you go up there one day
try and see with his eyes.

Autumn Afternoon

Big silence
here on the North Coast
a few miles up
from Thunder River

I drink the last of the whisky
watching the maple leaves
burn in the frosty light

I'm saying goodbye to something
but I don't know what.

                                      (Gulf of the St Lawrence)

Ungava

Ever listened to the wind?
ever listened to the ice?

ever listened to the wind on the ice?

that's Ungava

the name comes
from an Eskimo word: *ungawak*

'the farthest place'.

More News from Montreal

I was coming back to Montreal from nowhere North America
in a bus whose drone was made for long-distance meditation

the Laurentian woods were end-of-year red
the river was hyperborean blue

Yamaska
Drummondville
Rivière-du-Loup

the city's glass towers arose on the horizon
reflecting the postmo atmosphere

TERMINUS VOYAGEURS

'It's absolutely gorgeous, this weather
maybe we're going to have
a Florida winter'
(woman on the wistful sidewalk, Sherbrooke)

'René, my love, where are you?
the night is warm
we could wrap it around us
to make a paradise'
(on a sentimental wall in the Rue St-Antoine)

'We're at stagnation point'
(tough taxi-driver, Côte-des-Neiges)

the professor of human geography at UQAM
had a dreamcatcher dangling above his desk.

Point Omega Transit

> For the year 2000

'Plenty work, but not *mucho dinero*'
said the Dominican Republican, computer technician
roulette croupier on St Martin

a Sunday evening, in the month of Augusto
at the international airport of Santo Domingo

Tienda Colombo, Tienda Bolero

'watches, cameras, cigarillos
all cigarette
14 U.S. dollar or ten pound'

huge Patton ventilators on wheels
are busy stirring the heat around

the dulcet guff from the cafeteria
mingles with the stench of stale tobacco

Esencias del mundo

no use at all (you listening, Aristotle?)
in praying to Plato
or making out with the muses
(even if they come from Ipanema)
modo latino

while the commentators of these end times
serve up the same old classical themes
in current sociological sauce
the eminent exercise
is to move out
(like Cantor or Duns Scot)
from paradox to paradox

and from desolation to delight
on unedited tracks

the Air Britannia for Glasgow
(remember Strathbungo and Lesmahagoe?)
is rarin' to go

me, I'm making for Jericho
(the walls of the world are tumbling down)
and from there to paradisal points unknown

via the high plateaux of Mexico

OK, Santo Domingo
hasta luego, ciao.

A Short Walk among Primal Signs

1. *Ireland*
When the pine and the hazel
came out of the ice
you could hear on these marshes
the cry of the crane.

2. *Labrador*
Scratched on grey rock
by the crawling ice:
'What region is this
what shore of the universe?'

3. *Arizona*
This is how it all began
in the white and the yellow
the owl was hooting in the tree
as we made up North.

4. *Mexico*
In the blue of the evening
at the hour of the first star
the hunch-backed flute player
heads for the hills.

5. *Guadeloupe*
Wide open eyes
ghost faces
fixed here on the rock –
Arawak!

The Rainy Season on Martinique

In the immediate neighbourhood
the *thump-thump-thump*
and the *thump-thump-thump*
of zouk

but the tropical downpour drowns it all
and the roar of the wide Atlantic

while, in the clearings
look, the magnificent men-o'-war
ride, silently, the air.

News from the Islands

1.
Up the slope of Pelée, as you climb
you hear the Mountain Whistler, never see him.
(Martinique)

2.
The caiali sits on the mangrove tree, a scraggy little thing
then, *kio kio kio*, he's a fine bold heron on the wing.
(Guadeloupe)

3.
That screech on the crest of the hill country
was the migratory falcon, *gri-gri*.
(La Désirade)

4.
Puffins wailing in the night
as they fly north over Caye Plate.
(Marie-Galante)

5.
Coolicoo-coo-coo, coolicoo – the voice of love
listening all day long to a Zenaida dove.
(Anguilla)

Quiet Days on Guadeloupe

The morning began
with a solemn pelican fishing off the pier
I observed his long-beaked dive and skim
dive and skim

yelling terns excitedly cross and recross the skyline

(these are dry days on Guadeloupe
banana fronds hang limp and dying
their red-glistening stocks a pale and brittle brown)

the sea gulps in against the coraline rocks

the ferry to the Saints ploughs a dazzling white furrow
another follows on, bound for Marie-Galante

I watch them disappear over the horizon

with my back against the trunk of a flowering flamboyant
I'm reading a massively erudite study
on the habitat and habits of the geotrygon

involved in a kind of eternity
the days move on and on.

Memories of Indian River

Mangrove trees
with tressed and sworling roots

red-clawed crabs
staring from the rocks.

blue heron, green heron!

and the slickering sound of the prow
as it nosed its way slowly
up through the shadows.

         (Dominica, West Indies)

Semaphore Hill Soliloquy

Just before dawn
I heard thick rain
tumbling on the elephantine leaves of the grape-tree
now at nine
the Atlantic down there is a hazy blue
a warm wind
rustles over the promontory's dry forest
and a hummingbird is busily at work
on one luscious hibiscus flower after the other

once more on the island
in the brazilwood cabin
on the Caravelle peninsula
under the spidery pillars of the old semaphore
I work at a manuscript in the long quiet mornings
and in the afternoon visit the dark-entangled mangrove
or the furnace-red chaos of Devil's Point
in the twilight, savouring a mellow rum

I tell no stories
imagining maybe at most
the initial, pre-historical habitations:
migratory terns
a lizard arriving haphazard on a bit of driftwood...
after that, the noise begins
(I've read all about it
and have my opinions)

back to hibiscus and humming-bird
to the warm wind fondling the multi-leafed forest
to the glassyblue expanse of the Atlantic

and the manifold, semaphoric manuscript.

(Martinique)

Another Island Journey

Coming down to Sint-Maarten
through ten kilometres of thick blanket cloud

filling in the landing card
'Are you here for business?
For pleasure?
Are you on honeymoon?'

as usual, friend, just passing through

signs of the last cyclone everywhere to be seen
ripped up roofs, shattered palms
boats at all angles
including one battered red-funnelled oldtimer
The Carib Islands

from my rain-dripping balcony
I watch a grey pelican flying by nonchalantly
over the glaucousgreen waters.

The Anegada Passage*

Leaving Antigua six hours late
by the grace of LIAT

'your life-belt is under your seat
relax and enjoy the flight'

moving up to Tortola
on a Dehavilland Twin Otter

five in the afternoon
flying above the baroque cloud
in an azure-blue void

a chain of islands glimpsed in golden light:
Nevis, St Kitts, St Eustatia and Saba

beyond Anguilla, it's the Anegada Passage

wide and empty waters
Sombrero there lost to the North-East

you move down then to the Virgins
the intellect thinking of territories
between the end-time and the origins.

Seven Views of Virgin Gorda

1.
A horizon of hazy islands:
borne on the warm breeze
the cries of laughing gulls.

2.
Coming down the windy, wilderness path:
those old guardians of the garden
the green, milkyblue and crimson-fruited cacti.

3.
A shoal of lovely palometas
(paleblue-silver bodies, slender jetblack fins)
passes silently to larboard.

4.
Another delight of Devil's Bay:
in the total blue submarine dusk
nine medusae illumined by the morning sun.

5.
Evening in the archipelago:
within the space of an infinite sky
the Beef Island lighthouse blinking in and out.

6.
On the verandah, smoking a quintero
watching bluegrey cloud moving slowly
over the greyblue channel waters.

7.
A tropical wave moving fast West:
wind howling all around the house
sheets of rain blinding the windows.

In Praise of Pelicans

They make no noise
just sit long hours on a rock
looking down their nose

if a gannet comes along
they give the guy room
without making a song and dance about it

when they go out fishing
they let gulls clamber over them
and join in the act

never saying a word
they make back then for their rock
until finally, with no fuss at all, they call it a day.

(Anguilla, West Indies)

Companion of the Morning

The little kestrel

with her shrill wee trill
her unambiguous beak
her thick-feathered Robinson Crusoe thighs

is perched
high atop the old telegraph pole

all around her
a stretch of bushy wind-rustling wilderness
and the absolute azure of the skies

she is up there
totemly still

watching

like a hawk.

(Virgin Islands)

Farewell to an Island

I'll remember the path at dawn
lined with jagged blue cactus
and sweet-smelling white-flowered frangipani
winding down to the cove

I'll remember the clink of broken coral

I'll remember the choruses of laughing gulls
the plungings of pelicans
the silent passages of fishes
all the colours of the rainbow

I'll remember the warm breeze

I'll remember the evening skies
the great slashes of red across the green
and the signal-light on the headland
silverly blinking

I'll remember the sudden squalls

but what I'll remember most, perhaps, is this:
the shrill wee cry of the kestrel
over the wilderness.

(Virgin Islands)

Final Note

It was an old black woman
pottering about her scrubland garden
coming on sundown

I'd been asking about plants and herbs
she'd been telling me about properties and uses –
I had a notebook crammed with ethno-pharmaceutical
;information

then I pointed to a plant still unnoticed
low-lying, dark-leaved, blue-flowered
growing scatteredly along the wayside

'Oh, dat one', she said, 'dat's nuthin
dat's jus' a li'l ole weed dat's called *marron*'.

(Virgin Islands)

Way Back

Rubbing noses
across the Bering straits:
America and Asia.

Eastern Waters Again

South China Sea

1.
Half fish, the thread fish
alectis ciliaris
the other half sheer ecstasy.

2.
What does he see
the 'Japanese big eye'?
oceanic fujiyamas.

Autumn at Luk Wu Temple

1.
Twelve miles along the coast
now in the evening mist
the red gates.

2.
Why did Buddha come from the West?
– a bowl of noodles
and this amber-coloured tea.

3.
A temple in the mountains:
the sound of sweeping
the sound of sweeping.

4.
Wind in the pines
the roof-bell tolling
through the mosquito net: the moon.

5.
Leaving at dawn
after rice gruel and beans
the call of a wood-pigeon.

(Lantao Island, South China Sea)

Between Kaifeng and Kweiteh

Li Po's residence

Not exactly a monastery
but a lonely house standing by a river
his neighbour the kingfisher

brush galloping day after day
('ah, the many branchings of the way!')
downing bowl after bowl of amber wine
('the whole world is wholly in flux!')

looking at
brown stains on the bamboo, ancient tears

imagining
West of the great wall
sandy wastes strewn with bones
the bird-tracks of Szechwan

ghosts whistling in the rain.

The Lung-Shan Folk

Where we came from remains obscure
as also who and what we were

at one point, sure
we dwelt on the plains of Eastern China

there we made pottery
thin, fine and black

before moving on doggedly
into oblivion.

A Little Chinese Story

>   XIth century, Sung dynasty

Rich in gold
and in other minerals
the mountains
of Chen-si

numerous, the prospectors
eager to possess them

but in their wisdom
the authorities

considering
that the place's *fengshui*
its 'wind and water' lines
is still more precious

have forbidden all mines

the landscape is still breathing
the people's eyes are clear.

In the Mountains of Taiwan

Up here
there is neither East nor West
the white heron
has disappeared in the mist.

Stones of the Cloudy Forest*

In memoriam Hsiang Pi Fêng

1.
Where the path ends
the changes begin
and the rocks appear
ideas of the earth.

2.
Lying in the mist
among red rocks
admiring the lessons
of wind and rain.

3.
As the old man said
up in the mountains
close to the sky
every rock looks like a lotus.

Rangoon Rag

I have lived in the house of Rangoon Red
watching the lotus grow
let the Rangoon music run through my head
knowing all I needed to know.

(Night train, Bangkok–Chieng Mai)

Earth Dance

Red silk
red lips
red hands
red feet

red earth
red flame
red flow
red beat

red cool
red flower
red jewel
red lustre

after
take the dancer.

                (A night in the hills)

Autumn in Kyoto

1.
Across the wooden bridge
in the sunset –
the evening is full of echoes.

2.
Night in the ancient capital –
on the grey waters of the river
a white heron.

3.
Kyoto Tower:
the lighthouse
to an ocean of dreams.

4.
Red lips
in a rainy street:
the face of Autumn.

5.
Empty bamboo
and water trickling –
Ryoan-ji, early morning.

North Road, Japan*

1.
That autumn morning
on the waters of the Sumida
one lone gull.

2.
At Shirakawa
no poem, no song
only the rain.

3.
In the mountains
on the bank of a torrent
drinking cold saké.

4.
All alone
with an old crow
in unfamiliar territory.

5.
Sun
shining in a waterfall
oshara shonara.

6.
Green pine
growing on the heights
century after century.

7.
North country:
that bear print
on the post-office wall.

In the Straits of Tsugaru

Once again, outward bound

nihilistic gulls
crying in the wind

getting up into
that North-east corner of the mind.

Joseph Martin's Report

The expedition lasted
more than 6 months
we marched 125 days

the journey
was 2,500 versts long
on 600 of which
we had to hack our way
with axes

we lost
all the horses
and 7 dogs
2 men died
1 went mad

the land is beautiful.

                                        (Sikhote Alin Mountains)

Back on the Atlantic Line

Along the Atlantic line
in the blue of a May morning

(fellow travellers
playing Scrabble, reading the news
nobody looking out there at the land)

Rochefort, La Rochelle, La Roche-sur-Yon...

(last night in Bordeaux
at the bar of Pépé Gallego)

a sequence of rugged pinetrees, then
ah, the breathing emptiness of the sea.

Settling into Yet Another Place

1.
In the old house
the grey sparrows
talk with the brown mice.

2.
Red rocks
in the morning sun
and the calls of gulls.

3.
Getting on with the job
never saying a word –
the spider.

4.
White beach
on a summer morning
sea surfing up through mist.

5.
Blue evening light
over Lannion Bay –
I pull out the telephone plug.

6.
Misty evening on the docks:
that red-bellied fish
called 'the old woman'.

7.
Black, white-black, black-white-red:
a quick flight of oystercatchers
over the grey sea.

On the Quay at Lannion

There they were
on the quay at Lannion
mother and daughter
selling spider-crabs

big ones, real beauts
and I said
where were those fished from
our place, she said

at Paimpol
beyond the hollow rocks.

At Gwenved*

1.
Summer thunder
and a white butterfly
fluttering over the maize field.

2.
Early morning storm:
rain on the petunias
fine lightning in the bone.

3.
Something reddening out there
very quietly reddening –
they call it Autumn.

4.
An evening at Gwenved:
the red maize field
behind it, the roar of the sea.

5.
On the roof now only
one lone magpie
gazing at the mist.

Somewhere in Brittany*

An empty road

words
on a tattered poster:

Brezhoneg
Fest-Noz jusqu'à l'aube

three sparrows
in the cold raw rain.

The Old Sea-Chapel at Paimpol

Inside
religious rigmarole
but here on the grey stone wall
austere and plain
exposed to wind and sleet and rain
the ex-votos:

*In memory of Silvestre Bonnard
Captain of the sloop Mathilde
lost in Iceland*

*To the memory of Silvestre Camus
lost in the region of the Norden Fjord
in Iceland*

the eye moves on down the beach
where, on the shingle line
bulky and black
somebody's mending a boat.

Île de Bréhat

It was a man from here
told Christopher

how to get to the New World

I walk among grey stones
thinking of something without a name.

Goaslagorn

Little valley
full of yellow whin
for years and years
you've been a wilderness

now the committee
of 'sensitive areas'
wants to make a path through you
for people to walk on
down to the sea

okay, people
there's your path
be careful with it
(no cigarette packets, no beer bottles
no radios, please)
smell the whin
listen to the wind
go down to the sea
in peace.

Point to Point

1.
February wood
sound of my footsteps
on the frosted leafage.

    (Huelgoat)

2.
Along the ferny road
by the chapel of the Seven Saints
under the full moon.

    (Near Lannion)

Armorica

Under cloud-scudding sky
late Autumn

the sea out there greylygreen
quick-flecked with white

in a blue-shuttered Breton town

the Inn of the West Wind
Marylou Floch proprietor

Galettes de blé noir
Couscous maison 5 € la part

I sat in there for a while
listening to the conversation
looking out at the cloud

then left again
out on the road again
the old sea-road to Gwenadur.

Strathclyde

In memoriam William White

Early morning:
a cold light
blustering over the Firth

ten tolls
on Columba's clock

'nice morning, isn't it?'

the ferry
leaving for the islands

gulls
swarming round a fishing smack
out there
in the windy whiteness

'love dwells
along the margins of the sea
and in the mind'.

Aberdeen: a Pilgrimage

'Petrol capital of Europe'

A grey rain's falling over Trinity Quay

out beyond the harbour
('The entrie is somewhat difficult
because of a sand bed
comonelie called the Barre')
the North Sea
is grinding, whining and howling

here however in *The Schooner*
they're making an enticing offer
of whisky, vodka, dark rum, gin
and, on Sunday at noon
(God help the poor old pastor)
'Exotic Girls; join in the fun'

you can also
get yourself a classy tattoo:
maybe the Chinese ideogram for 'demon'?

DEEP FREEZE SUPPLIES

at three of the morning
in the *Gordon Arms*
(that displays on its wall
the 'Scotland for ever!' charge at Waterloo)
Arctic gulls
glide ghostily by the window.

A Letter from Wisconsin

It comes in an almost
illegible scrawl

from N. 85th Street
Wauwatosa, Wisconsin

and I wonder
what crazy man's written it

full of American intellectualese

'the sinews of entropy
congruency to my reality'

yet it pleases me, it
pleases me well

there's a wild coolness
back of the jargon

a man's voice in Wisconsin
in the silence under Orion.

Good News out of Russia

A birdwatcher
sends me it
straight out of Siberia

a tiny wee tin thing
(seminar badge)
at the centre

two rosy gulls on the wing.

Flotsam

On a Breton shore
this autumn morning

a plank of pine

W: 22 kilos
M: 122 x 24 x 22 mm

these data are specified

beside them
half-effaced
these words:

Captain
ship
Nagasaki, Japan.

Heard on the Moor

Evening twilight
on the moors of Lanvaux:
'waste land, wan land
moor always goes back to moor'.

Autumn at Gwenved

1.
Early October:
in the morning mist
Korean chrysanthemums.

2.
A crow
skimming over the sea-rocks?
the shadow of a gull.

3.
On the frost of the garden
the paw-prints of the cat
on his way to the woods.

4.
This evening over Gwenved
at the setting of the sun
every gull is a rosy gull.

5.
All the stillness
of that autumn morning
was on the wings of the dragonfly.

On the Promontory

They're talking up in The Hague:

'In 1900 the Himalaya had ten thousand glaciers
now two thousand less

the ice-cover of the Alps
has been cut by two in the last century and a half

the Alaska glacier
has gone down by twenty per cent over the last fifty years'

the planet, they say, is warming up
we can expect storm and flood

a lot of low-lying land is going to disappear

it's already happening

I'm sitting here
on one of Europe's rocky promontories
listening to the tide
watching the cloud.

Meditant

It was the cold talk of the gulls he liked
and rain whispering at the western window
long days, long nights
moving in
to what was always nameless
(though the walls were hung with maps
and below him
lay a library of science)

Outside
at the end of that dark winter
he saw blue smoke, green waters
as he'd never seen them before
they were enough
a black crow busy on a branch
made him laugh aloud
the shape of the slightest leaf
entertained his mind
his intellect
danced among satisfactory words.

Getting Things Ready for the Guest

Swab the windows
(six months of bird shit
spattered mud and salty rain)
till they're clear
diamond-clear

enter now a magpie
in Chinese: 'bird of joy'
chack-chack, chack-a-chack
all over the garden

put the white wine in ice

that's it –
now just sit.

BOOK VII

Leaves of an Atlantic Atlas

'Atlantic' is geographical, but also multidimensional. Atlantic as magnitude and extent, scope and flow. The Atlantic as approach to Open World Ocean. Time yielding to space: cartography. Maybe this whole section is something like a *magna carta geopoetica*.

Venetian Notes

Universis et singulis

1. *On the roof of the Londra Palace*

Ah, that mixed and multiple movement!

lighters, launches, ferries
crissing and crossing
gondolas tossing at their moorings
and a massive tanker from Istanbul
being tugged, slowmotionly, down the glowing Giudecca Canal

above all the mellow tolling
of San Giorgio's bell.

2. *In the Basilica*

Sea-city, open city

where Mark arrived on a square-sailed barque
and Pelagius came flying in
on the blue wings of a storm
city of billowing floors
and cloudy marble

city of a floating dream.

3. *At the prow of the Dogana*

Tide-slap against wood and stone
gulls of the Adriatic
wheeling and screaming
in the windy brightness

OK, il prezzo e giusto

maybe, as a curious contribution

to the nomadic and geopoetic library
I should have bought that
*Sketchbook of an American
in the year 1860*
offered by the antiquary...

4. *In the gardens*

It is possible the Oversoul
is *'irgendwie nordisch'*
as the professor from Hamburg
remarked in the trattoria

a weatherbeaten Pluto
eyes a pockmarked Proserpine

I lie out on a bench
beside a flowering viburnum.

5. *On the Isola San Pietro*

In the alleys and rios
lights and shadows
lines of multicoloured washing

on a cobbled piazzale
a woman shares out gobs of meat
to a tribe of thirty cats

all thin, wide-eyed, and wild.

6. *At the Doge's Palace*

Keeping an eye
over sea and land

commissions, promissions
written out in a clear hand

English ambassadors arriving
(try not to look too bored)

how to marry wave and word.

7. *At Torcello*

You board the vaporetto
at the Fondamenta Nuove

Murano breathes fierce heat
and displays cool glass

you pass San Giacomo in Palude
and the lace-making island of Burano

calm waters, patches of fenland
gull-country

when you come off the n° 12 at Torcello
the sun that was white is now a red glow

a cathedral on an island
bewildered, abandoned

a trilling of birds, a wandering cat
an old man rowing a boat.

8. *Hôtel window, evening*

Night falling
voices fading from the quays
gondoliers covering their barques

and suddenly, all along the lagoon
the lighting up of the hidden channels.

9. *A dream of ships*

Egyptian river-boats
nestled in reeds

flatboats, like floating leaves
on the lake of Nemi

triremes and quinqueremes
rhythmic, determined

Phoenician boats craftily eyeing their way
through the mist of an uncharted sea...

Codex Oceanicus

1. *Tunis, 898*

The Uquiyanus
which is also called
the All-embracing Sea
the Green Zone
or the Sea of Darkness
is the sea of the Maghreb

it goes from the tip of Abyssinia
all the way up to Bartiniya

enormous waves
awful winds, fearsome storms
all kinds of monsters
islands as numerous as the stars

(it is said
eight men of Lisboa
blown off their course
sailed eleven days
till they came to a place
under thick cloud
a faint light hovering
over jagged rock)
no wise ship will sail over such wan waters.

2. *The old man of Dieppe*

Before Henry the Navigator
sent down his Portugees in droves
to *aquellas partes do mar Ouciano*
there were other people on the job
down there on the coast of Africa

as early as 1280
two Genoese, Doria and Vivaldo
tried to make a journey
novo et inusitato
that is, to go to India
via the sea of Guinea –
bad luck stopped them in their tracks
but they reconnoitred the terrain
down there by Aguilon and Noun

a Spanish begging friar
with itchy feet
wandered down into that territory
and wrote a book about it

two Portugees
João Gonçalves Zarco
and
Tristão Vaz Teixeyra
tried to advance beyond Cape Bojador
but got caught in a storm
glad to find an island haven
they called Porto Santo

a Majorcan
by the name of Ferrer
(they tell of this on a Catalan portulan)
got as far as the River of Gold

we, I mean the Normanders
we were down there in the early 1300s
along by White Cape
and Boulombel

dropping in on
the Isle of Goats, the Isle of Doves

the Isle of Cormorants

we traded on the beaches
with the Ethiopians
traded for gold, ivory and amber

I remember burning sand
but also rain and wind
for months on end

all this was before the big days of slavery
before the colonizers came in
before the shit hit the fan

a lot was going on
but it was outside history.

3. *Antillia*

A study looking over the bay
near the Doge's Palace
full of maps, books, and manuscripts

in it, at work on his atlas
Andrea Bianco, Venetian
registered in the Archives of the Republic
as *ammiraglio, uomo di consiglio*
master of merchant galleys
on the routes to the Black Sea
as to the Barbary Coast, Beirut, Alexandria

but mostly, in his heart of hearts, cartographer

on his first sheet of vellum
(29 centimetres by 38)
he'd described the Rule of Martelio
for resolving a course

on the second
he'd traced the coasts of the Black Sea
which he knew from close acquaintance

likewise, on sheets three and four
for the coast of the East and Central Mediterranean

now on sheet five
after Spain, Portugal, North Africa
he was drawing in the Atlantic Islands

the Azores, all clear and defined
the same for Madeira and the Cabo Verde

but then...

he took another glance at Pizzigano's map
and gazed out over the bay

everybody in Venice knew the Portuguese story
of those priests who
when the Arabs overran Iberia
had fled out into the ocean
founding seven cities on an unknown island
called 'Antillia'

but it was all as loose and vague
as the Isle of Brandan

for a moment he wavered
then thought 'to hell'
and painted it in

after all, it was always *possible.*

4. *Leonardo's testament*

I learned how to make all kinds of instruments

I manufactured machines
so they could wage their stupid wars
with greater efficiency

I mastered the art of painting
and did at least one portrait
that will keep them guessing for centuries

I could even compose respectable poems

but none of all this
really touched me deeply
my best, my most exploratory work
was done in my notebooks
written the wrong way round
(to read them, they'll need a mirror)
and often enough with the left hand

there my thought pushed me on and on
and in all directions

at times I'd cut into the flux
to make separate studies:
'On the nature of water'
'On tides', 'On clouds'
'On the flight of birds'
but all idea of organization
in the absence of new, generalizing concepts
soon became hopeless

Michelangelo couldn't understand
why a good painter
should 'waste his time'
on such *ghiribizzi*
but Michelangelo, well
he was an excellent artist, hardly more

I hear them now jabbering
about their Great New World
the transatlantic dream
but the real new world
the cosmo-chaotico-poetical universe
lies in my *ghiribizzi*.

5. *Samuel Champlain writing from the Virgins*
It all began in Brittany, in 1598

I'd come up from the South-West
with the army of our Henry
to take part as quartermaster
in the taming of that wild country

the campaign over
I found myself unemployed –
decided then to go down to Spain

the Spaniards were at Blavet
where they'd build a fort
so was one of my uncles, Captain Provençal
commissioned by the King of Spain as pilot-general

we left the Breton coast in early August
and twenty days later were at Sanlucar
at the mouth of the Guadalquivir
that's where I had some chance
of finding a ship for the Indies
(so as to make enquiries into matters
of which as yet no Frenchman
had managed to obtain cognizance)

on the third day of January, 1599
we made out into the Atlantic
with a steady cutting wind

after nine weeks
we came in view of the island
Columbus called the Deseada
then moved up farther North
to a hundred scattered islets
all desert and uninhabited
from where I'm writing now

the sea this evening is greyly green
with copper splashes on the horizon
it looks as if tomorrow will bring rain.

Isolario*

Prologue
The accomplished pilot
knows the way of the stars
can read the signs
be they regular or accidental
recognizes exactly where he is
by the fish he sees
the colour of the waters
the depths he sounds
he has an excellent memory
is in full possession of his powers
can stand heat, rain or cold
that's why he's called
'the man who gets to the other shore'.

1.
A volcanic rock
all alone in the ocean

great lizards
living on grass

strange birds.

2.
This is the zone of dry rain
out from the desert of Africa
borne by the harmattan

among the red and yellow ash
a little grey-leaved lavender.

3.
Fields of lava
steamy air
moss-covered slopes

among the ruined walls
of a rank garden
a tulip tree and an araucaria

when the west wind starts to blow
make for shelter.

4.
Nobody lives here
nobody
but *cagarra* gulls.

5.
On this island
you'll find a line of white dunes
made of broken shell

the plants that grow there
look like branches of coral.

6.
Lava flows here unceasingly

sometimes fast as water
sometimes slow as honey.

7.
Out from the land of the Abyssinians
it's an unknown sea and wide

if you cross right over
you come to the red lands of Komor.

8.
In these islands
when the monsoon blows
the thunder lasts for days

lightning leaps
from ridge to ridge

the forest
bows and sways in the rain

but away up there
in the depths of the sky
shines a crystalline blue.

9.
Between the Laquedives and the Maldives
stands an island
shaped like a crescent moon

its beach is littered
with white cowrie shells.

10.
Near the isle of Sanchâo
you'll see the following signs:
a flight of gannets
and floating masses of sargasso weed.

11.
Here lies Fernâo Mendes
author of a *Peregrinaçâo*
which he wrote
with the feather of an albatros
on the island of Pulo-Chapalo
away down the China Sea.

Fragments of a Logbook

Date uncertain

1.
On the 15th day of November
we saw, off to starboard
a lonely rock.

2.
Black hulk
its outlines
suggesting roughly
the body of a crow

staring
you could almost hear it caw.

3.
On our charts
are five sea-provinces
clearly marked:

the arctic
the boreal
the celtic
the lusitanian
the mediterranean

we lie here now
on the line
that joins the celtic to the boreal.

4.
We've begun by studying
the distribution of species
in the tidal zone

several seaweeds:
fucus serratus
rhodomenia palmata
himanthalia lores
laminaria flexicaulis
saccorhiza bulbosa

among the shells:
patella vulgata
dosinia exoleta
venus verrucosa

several starfish
of the *asterias glacialis* family

and a crab:
xanthus floridus

tomorrow
we'll climb
to the island's peak.

5.
On a rock
engraven
these two signs:
K
*
(according to our linguist
runes:

ka
who knows the secrets
hagal
the universe).

6.
Up there
nothing
not even bones
only rock
wind
and boundless sea.

7.
All night
with my eyes
following the star

all night
sailing in the sky.

8.
Abrupt and brutal
like
nothing at all

the thing to be said.

9.
kraa, kraa

dark isle
black bird

kraa, kraa

root tongue
back of time

kraa, kraa

place of memory
and apocalypse.

The Western Gateways*

Prologue
From a crystal window at Saint-Jean-de-Luz
I look out on the Western Seas

listening to the winds:
enbata, the sea breeze
ipharra, the northerner
iduzki-haizea, the wind of the sun
hegochuria, the hot south wind
haize-belza, the dark northwesterly

thinking of the sea of the philosophers
but also of whales and whalemen.

1.
Straw fires lit
all along the coast

smoke signals

drums beating and voices shouting
'*baleak berriz etorri dira!*'
(the whales are back)

quick, the harpoons

boats out from Biarritz
Socoa and Guéthary

strike!

hauling in the great fat monsters

blood baths, piles of blubber

whale tongue broiling and sizzling
in the little houses of Bayonne.

2.

They'd turn up in the Gulf
about the time of the autumn equinox
and were plentiful from January to May

not sperms, or big blues
but the *baleine franche*
the *baleine des Basques*

what the Basques themselves called *sardaka*
and the Hollanders *nord-kapper*

balena borealis.

3.

Many a fisherman's cottage
along that basque and gascon coast
had whale bones for rafters

if you lay to rest under such a roof
you saw whales in your sleep!
and when you woke
there were whales in your prayers:

Que Diou ens préserbi
dou cantic de la sirène
dou coudic de la balène
et dou clouché de Mimizan

4.

Came a day
when the whales no longer appeared in Biscay
(because they'd got wise to the Basques
or because of some cosmic change
that had nothing to do with men?)

at Guéthary, they waited
at Bayonne, Biarritz and Saint-Jean-de-Luz
but the whales stayed away

nothing to do but go after them.

5.

A hundred boats left every year
every year in the month of March
they'd set out from the Biscay harbours

by April-May they were off the Labrador

Vrolicq of Saint-Jean-de-Luz
drew a map of 'Arctic France'
marking the hunting grounds:
Cap de Biscaye, Baie des Basques...

one big fish after another
got a kiss from a Basque harpoon

they built ovens on the beaches
melted down the tons of fat
loaded it into sturdy barrels
and brought it all back home.

6.

Other peoples got into the act

like the Bretons of Saint-Malo
Paimpol and the Île de Bréhat

men from Le Havre and La Rochelle
Dutchmen, Englishmen, Russians, Danes

but if you were after a firstrate harpooner
you still went down to the South-West

the Whaling Company of London
had a recruiting agent at Saint-Jean-de-Luz
the Dutchman Van Muyden, alias Le Flamand
hired twelve Basque sailors at Saint-Jean
including three harpooners

when the *Elizabeth*, captain Jonas Poole
and the *Mary Margaret*, captain Steven Benet
sailed from Liverpool in 1612
they had six Basque harpooners on board:

Jean de Bacogne
Juan de Aguerre
Martin de Karre
Marsine de Horisada
Domingo de Sarria
Adam de Belloka

wild men, every man jack of them

wasn't it said a Basque harpooner
would take a leap on to the whale's broad back
to make sure the dart was well lodged?!

7.
Cleirac, *Us et coutumes de la mer*
describes the harpoon:

'*grand javelot de fer battu
emmanché sur un bois très solide
à la pointe acérée et tranchante
triangulaire en fer de sagette
portant gravée au bout haut
la marque du ministre*'

I saw one years ago in a Dutch museum

the name it bore was
Michelanz de Cubibure
(which must be Ciboure).

8.

Were there any philosophical whalemen
on the misty coasts of America?

Williams (William Carlos) evokes
'the raw beauty of ignorance
that lies like an opal mist
over the West coast of the Atlantic
beginning at the Grand Banks
and extending into the recesses of our brains'

did any of those wild men feel this?

or were they only concerned
with heaving their heavy harpoon
and melting down that bubbling blubber?

some of them must have felt it
even if they couldn't say it.

9.

They sang songs:

Pour la grande pêche baleinière
Et pour la chasse aux cachalots
Ont signé l'rôle au commissaire
Vingt-cinq lascars, fins matelots
Sont descendus tous en troupeau
Aux maisons closes d'la rue Rouleau
...
Avez-vous vu dans Rotterdam
Écoutez bien c'que j'vas vous dire

La belle Annie qui fut ma femme
Et m'a damné pour son sourire
    Embarque le mou au galant
    Car la barque roule au vent
...
En revenant de La Rochelle
Pique la baleine, joli baleinier
J'ai rencontré Mam'zelle Hélène
Pique la baleine, joli baleinier
Allons naviguer...

10.

I imagine a silent harpooner
(his mates think he has no fun)
taking it all in

he sees the white fat in the whale's great brain
he sees the she-whale's milk
thick as mayonnaise

he watches the blue mists rolling on the Labrador

he listens to the Indians talking
and the Eskimo talking
using a kind of pidgin basque

he feels the hugeness of it all
and the grotesque reality of it all

he lives with the vision and the savour of it all

(his mates think he has no fun).

11.

Strange memories lurk in his skull

and when he looks at the Milky Way

he sees ancient pilgrimages

all the starry places along the Pyrenees
Venus advancing along the way
more and more naked with every step

taking the soul to the white lands
gate after gate

seven gates in all
the way of the wild geese

he cannot get it all into focus
but those strange memories go with him.

12.

I imagine him also
(oh, he is a strange one)
burning the midnight oil
(a fat candle of whale fat)
and poring over Seneca
(he learned Latin, for fun
from a priest in Bayonne):
'a day will come
when men will find
the great secret hidden in the ocean'

these words he underlines
thinking.

13.

Hey, down there
she blows!

blow! blow!
blow! blow!

boats out

quiet
she sounds

quiet

quiet

stand up!

strrrike!

In the Sand Parishes

Begin, say, with Brouage

grey ramparts
looking out over the marshes
the cry of a linnet
above the oyster-beds
a chill wind blowing from the West

walk around the almost empty streets
('the young folk are leaving the place
who can blame them?')
till you come to that pillar
bearing the worn white globe

inside the church
(damp and cold, the whitewashed walls)
on a stained-glass window
you will read these lines:

The sea has withdrawn
like history from the land
and the unknown fortress
lives now only
thanks to the passing wind

here Champlain prayed
before leaving once more for Hochelaga
where only the wind now blows
over the sanded harbour...

move then farther South
down by Spanish Point
along that coast
where the Phoenician boats slipped past

on the tin road to Cornwall

go down by Royan
cross the sand-coloured waters of the Gironde
and the vineyards of Medoc
(Theon lived there in a reed-roofed hut)
till you come to that chain
of silent villages
where the sand piles up
against bleached wood
and dune grass
waves in the ocean wind
(long rollers combing in over the beaches)

walk there
in that emptiness
full of sunlight

thinking of so many places
so many traces

lost in the sand.

The Ocean Way[*]

Travelling up the coast
that brightblue autumn morning
with a head full of Irish whiskey
(a certain drunkenness makes thought come easier)

'what matters', I was saying to myself
'nothing human, that's sure'

it was one of those supernihilistic journeys
only an extravagant Scot
or maybe a Greek or a Russian
can know

'*bonjour, beauté*', I said
in passing, to the world

sea-cloud in the sky

ozeanisches Gefühl

Bordeaux
Bourse maritime, Dansk Konsulaat
Bar de la Gironde, Le Tampico, Atlantic Bar

a whiff of dark-red wine

and the big river
mother-of-waters
flowing slowly West
in a golden haze

MAMAN ROSE

FOIE GRAS

farewell to Gascogne

it was September
red apples
all along the road

night gathering
the waves darkening

kingfisher!

a round white moon
over La Rochelle

on the Place de l'Ancre
an electric guitar
and a slim girl singing
L.A. Woman

wind in the tamaris
cool wind in the tamaris

'Don't bogart that joint, my friend
pass it over to me'

red lamp out on the harbour waters

next morning
the flat lands of Vendée
low houses, marshes
fish, oysters, salt
white wind
white light

'what whiteness
will you add to this whiteness?'

high bridge over the Loire
at Saint-Nazaire

CHANTIERS DE L'ATLANTIQUE

La Roche-Bernard:
a full-sailed yacht
coming silently down the Vilaine
between the steep rock banks

eros, logos, cosmos

Armorican territory
the dumnonian coast

a sea-shaken house

salutations to Duns Scot
Scotus Erigena
and old Pelagius

vita maxima contemplativa

at the swirling centre
fire-wave, lightning-flower.

The Armorican Manuscript*

1.
Leaving the world
to its bickering and bargaining
he came over to Armor
across miles of metaphor

to the final door.

2.
To the East
the rising sun

to the South
red moors

to the West
the great coast

to the North
white fields.

3.
Rough rock
in the times of all that
hollow talk
rough rock edges, and
swirling
white sleek water
a wind-water place
with its curves and its cries
ora maritima
estuaries and tides
wings, waves, sands
rain and light.

4.
He liked the old tongue
with its rocky sounds:

'*War an dervenn pa bar al loar
bep noz 'n em zastum evned-mor*

*Evned-mor du o fluñv ha gwenn
gant ul lommig gwad war o fenn*

*Ganto ur Vranez gozh du-lovet
ganti ur Vran yaouank kevret*

*Skuizh o daou ha gleb o eskell
o tonet eus tramor, eus pell*

*Hag an evned a gan ur c'han
ken kaer ma tav ar mor ledan*'.

5.
'*Bran*,' he thought
looking at the cormorant
drying its wings
in the morning sun
– and it was Megara, that promontory:
marine semantics
thalassic philosophy.

6.
He often dipped into the little book
of Marban the hermit:

'Birds come, bright and fair
herons, gulls
it's no sad music
the sea brings here

and brown grouse
out of red heather

noise of wind
through branchy wood
grey cloud, water
falls
cry of swan
fine music'.

7.
Out there
no circus

only watching
and listening to the place

far away from noise
and from nuisance

worshipping
monotony and silence

novice of emptiness.

8.
Walking deliberately
on the great white beach
he recalled his Latin

ineffabilis fatus
inaccessibilis accessus
incorporalis corpus
superessentialis essentia
illocalis localitas
infiniti definitio

incircumscripti circumscriptio

'the road to paradise
is paved with paradox'.

9.
Out, in clear fact, beyond culture:

chaos surviving
in the rock's red veins
(silent gull
gliding
over thin white sand).

10.
It wasn't his voice
but he liked the old songs
that held the soul of the place:

'The rain is falling
on the Arrée hills
the rain is falling
on the shores and fells

The rain is falling
on Cape Fréhel
the rain is falling
on the woods of Huel

The rain is falling
on the Isle of Ouessant
the rain is falling
on the roofs of Port-Blanc

The rain is falling'.

11.
Over on the headland
where the wind, from second to second
turns into light

he felt
a sense of living
at the edge of all knowing.

12.
Sometimes
he'd have a crack
with the ancient folk:

'Merlin, old Merlin
where go ye this mornin'
with your holly stick
and your big black dog?

yoo hoo, yoo hoo!'

I seek the red egg
of the great sea-snake
I seek the green cress
and the golden grass

yoo hoo, yoo hoo!'

13.
And the crows
those ragged rabbis

told apocalyptic stories
in the beech's branches.

14.
He liked the wild tales
that stand on the border
between two worlds:

'Near the forest of Caniscan
lives the hermit Iscolan

Seven years he's been out in the wind
for that he sinned

He sleeps on the barest stone
the poor man, Iscolan

When the grass is alive with fire
it's Iscolan's desire

A little book is all he wants
to be free of those wild haunts

The wee book's in the gob of a cod
that swims deep in the sea of God'.

15.
On the hawthorn path
that went down to the bay
(a labyrinth
of glimmer and shade)
he liked to feel
the clarity
gradually unveil –
till it came at him suddenly
with the beat of the wind.

16.
The boat he sailed
it was easy to recognize:

that high bow
with very marked sheer
and full-cheeked stem
the peak of the mainsail
high above the mast
boom extending well beyond stern.

17.
Sometimes out at sea
he'd sing himself a shanty song:

'*Sur l'île de Saint-Malo
je connais un matelot
qu'a fait le tour du monde
de Brest à Bornéo*

Sur son bateau la Blonde
*il voguait sur les flots
pour faire le tour du monde
d' Moscou à Macao*

*L'a vu la terre entière
l'a vu le bout du monde
épousé une bergère
sur les îles de la Sonde*

*À l'âge de cent deux berges
l'est revenu à Saint-Malo
pour rêver à des vierges
d'Oslo, d'Acapulco*'.

18.
In the blue morning mist
off the coast
that rock the seabirds
had covered
with immaculate shit...

he never tired
of watching it.

19.
Saying to himself:

where goes the world?
to the white

where goes the white?
to the void

where goes the void?

the void comes and goes
like the light.

Broken Ode to White Brittany*

And we're out
once again
on the transhuman road

*

A nation?
a country?

broken coastlines

here
no one talks
about States

*

'Dull weather', they tell me
they don't hear the gulls laughing whitely

*

Brest
midnight
in the Dead Man's Bar:
'another shot of that lousy red!'

*

Suddenly
here I am
in the Glasgow Road

and three mad ghosts
walking by my side

*

Introduced as a poet

he talked supernihilism

*

Down by the harbour:

sun-
light playing on the prow
of the *Agios Ioannis,* Famagusta

*

Anonymous archipelago

blue breakings

confused clarities

*

Reading beyond the legends

*

Enough
enough of that, enough of those

this wave breaking
white prose

*

May it never, don't forget
smell the poet

*

At last a little realness
this taste of salt on the tongue

*

White mist
at Roscoff

the outgoing tide

at Douarnenez

*

When they said: writing
he said: opening

*

Write poems?
rather follow the coast
line after line

going forward

breathing

spacing it out

*

Geographical calligraphy

*

This emptiness
that laughs at everything

all except *that*

*

Over against the -logies
of the logos gone dry

those two words:
sunt lumina

*

On the ridge of Trévézel

between rough grass
and black stone

*

All those
looking for a key
when all the time there's no door

*

At the Pointe du Van
this dawn

brain full of waves

*

That

to see it
get back into space

*

Played out
all the dialectics

*

High praise of pelagian space

*

Sunday morning at Plouguerneau

a gull crying
over the mass

'When Finn was alive, and the Fianna
moor and sea
meant more than any church'

*

The arrow
on the lighthouse

E-W

white wind.

The House at the Head of the Tide*

Five miles out of town
you come to a place called
the White Field

two wings and a whiteness
(ideogram for 'perseverance')

moorland, a rocky coast
and a hundred islands
the sea often green, gurly green
but every now and then
a sharp, breath-catching blue
with always breakers

peace, peace in the breakers

a place, this, of darkness and of light
darknesses and lights
in quick succession
the sun reveals, cloud conceals
and always a music
of wind on moor, tide on shore
and a silence

a fifth quartet

'we must be still
and still moving
for a further union
a deeper communion
through the dark cold
and the empty desolation
the wave cry, the wind cry
the vast waters
of the petrel and the porpoise'

a country lane lined with gorse
this house of stone
lined with a thousand books
that speak of ideas, islands
according to an order
as yet only dimly apprehended
vaguely sensed

chaoticism

where are we?
where are we going?
one who has thought his way
through the thicket
says it is a question of
moving into a new place
a clearing
we speak here in terms of
atlantica
a breathing and a breadth

pelagian space:
what was left out and behind
when the roads were built
and the codes of command
crammed into the mind
what was left out
becoming more and more
faintly articulate

still there in the gull cry
the wave clash
those darknesses, those lights
(but who hears? who sees?
who can say?)

another mindscape

moving out then
into the landscape
walking
in the white of the morning

walking and watching
listening

yellow flowers
tossing in the wind
a crow on a branch
caw-cawing
the rivulet
reflecting the sky
in blue-grey ripples
white beach, wrack
the high gait and snootiness
of oyster-catchers
a blue crab groping in a pool
bright shell

the notes accumulate

towards a writing
that has more in view
than the art of making verse
out of blunt generalities
and personal complaining

atlantic archipelago
and a sense of something
to be gathered in

the mind gropes
like a blue crab in a pool

tosses in the wind
reflects the sky in ripples
flies high
leaves signs in the sand
lies recklessly strewn
at the edge of the tide

comes back to the books
the many manuscripts

scriptorium
in candida casa
altus prosator

binoculars focused also
on the red-roofed
abandoned sardine-factory
at the tip of the promontory –
some kind of homology

a place to work from
(to work it all out)
a place in which to
house a strangeness

this strange activity
(philosophy? poetry?
practice? theory?)

from an accumulation of data
to the plural poem

beyond the generality.

Ovid's Report*

> On the shores of the Black Sea
> first century of our era

And they cast me out on the Scythian coast...

At first I found it hard to swallow
just imagine, me
Publius Ovidius Naso
one of Rome's brightest lights
well in with Horace and Propertius
a member of the Academy
alone among uncouth clods
on the cold and foggy banks
of the impossible Black Sea

I spat protest
the stench of swine and seaweed
offended my delicate nostrils
I scratched out elegies
finely wrought discourses
all to no good

In fact, strangely, in time
I found exile to my liking

Divorced from clique and public
with nobody to clap applause
at my capricious wit
I was able
to move off into the dark
and live with it

Between the pigs and the gulls
with no glib talk gliding off my tongue

I was no longer Naso
ad nauseam
the citizenship of Rome
dropped off me
like some old skin
the Midland Sea
suddenly looked wearisome
polluted, overpopulated
its *dolce vita*, insipid
the world opened up
wider and more demanding
than I'd thought

One day
thanks to some frozen river
barbarian hordes
will sweep down over the Latin lands
rushing to meet their future:
civilised primitives
sick of themselves –
I've gone the other way
I've come up North
where I fill my expanded lungs
with a sharper air

Here we are at the world's edge
a land of wind and shadow
on the banks of this rolling obscurity
a place of storm
and hard to navigate:
shallow waters
with short, quick, jabbing
waves

thick fog rising over them
through it at times you'll hear
a wild swan whooping

A long time, long ago
on the docks at Marseilles
in a tavern I met
a sailor from Greece
(Demosthenes was his name)
for a jar or two
he gave me a map –
for years and years
it lay forgotten
but I found it again in my papers
the day I left Rome
since then
it's been my favourite reading

Here's Europe
bound on the South by the Mediterranean
on the West by the Atlantic
on the North by the Sea of Britain
on the East
by the Danube and the Don

We all know Europe (or think we do)
we know Iberia
Celtia, Germania
and the isles of Britannia
we even know Thule
at least, by hearsay
but where we are now
everything's uncertain
all we've got is a host of questions

Big rivers
moving
through the night of the world:
the quickflowing Ister
that never freezes
the crystal-clear
Borysthenes
and the Tanaïs
wide and calm

This is Scythian land
an erratic, paradoxical people
bold as hell
dying with a laugh on their lips
and mourning the birth of babes
they're tattooed from head to toe
and swill beer
from the skulls of their kin

Up there
towards the sea of ice
roam the Hyperboreans
(unless of course they're just pure myth...)
between the Scythians and the Hyperboreans
a hundred peoples, a thousand tribes
Rome has never heard of:
the Gull Folk
the Star-seekers
the Seal-hunters
the People of the Mist
the Sons of the Wind
the Lonely Ones
the Stone Folk
and so on

ever more and more strange
those who wear shadows
those who fish in emptiness

Beyond the Caspian to the North
a land with no fixed limits
gripped in frost
to the East
the long dusty acres of Asia...

Outside the pale
rusticated once and for all
I went (abstractly) native
in art and in love
what I've always been after
and rarely found
was what would take me
the farthest possible out of myself

I've had enough, more than enough
of the all-too-human scene
that stuffy theatre
with its antics and its gestures
all those stories told and told again
what I'm interested in now
are the silent fields
I feel spreading all around me
the movements of the sea
the star-bespattered sky
the relation
between a body and the universe
the nebulae and a brain

I've known storms of the mind
sidereal emotions

intellectual auroras
as if the universe and myself
were one:
I've been
the flight of a crow
I've been
a shower of rain

I take quick notes
like this:
winter morning light
and a black-winged gull
keening over the hut –
no more than that
no metaphor-mongering
no myth-malarkey

I think of lines
like lightning flashes
lines that in their flying energy
would make things
touch and radiate in the mind

I'll have to be going farther
into this night
get further into
this new space
follow right through
the transhuman road
find, who knows, the source
of another light.

Brandan's Last Voyage*

Entendez ci de saint Brandent
Qui fu nez devers occident
Qui VII ans erra par la mer
Por plus douter Dieu et amer...

1.
It was a stony kingdom
on the West coast of Ireland
with the wind wailing
and the roaring of Atlantic breakers
with strange men wandering and murmuring:
is é mo drui Crist mac Dé
'my druid is Christ the son of God'.

2.
One had always wished to wander farther
Brandan by name and a name it was
that had the sea in it
the breaking of waves and the memory of a poem
the old men would speak on winter nights:
'Bran thinks a great marvel it is
to sail a boat on the clear sea
Bran's eyes see the waves of the sea
the sea waves shine in summer
as far as the eyes of Bran can see
Bran loves to look upon the sea
the white sea broken by oars'.

3.
There are men who are always ready
to throw everything to the winds
men who can look on life coldly

and stake everything on a gesture
Brandan was one of those
God for him was the great gesture
that had set everything in motion
also a great idea sailing through space
brighter than the sun and the moon.

4.
Brandan built him a boat

he built it of seventeen pieces
making first a framework of pliant wood
covering it with bull hides tanned in oak
smearing the hides with grease and resin –
a boat light as a bird to ride the sea!

when the boat was ready, firm and true
he gathered men about him, saying:
'this will be no pleasure cruise
rather the wildest of wild goose chases
around the rim of the world and farther
a peregrination in the name of God
and the promise of white martyrdom'.

5.
They pulled away from Ireland, heading North
oars dipping into blue water
amid a caterwauling of gulls

the going was good and the rhythm sure

to the East was the land of the white hills
and they passed by Islay, and the Isle of Tiree
then Barra, the Uists, till they came to Lewis

at the isle of Lewis they went ashore

walked round the ancient stones of Callanish
then headed again for the open sea.

6.
The weather went grey and the sea grew gurly
long days of rain, snow, sleet and wind
(surely this must be the very mouth of hell)
Brandan at the prow, crying into the greyness
is é mo drui Crist mac Dé!
the words lost in the grey wastes

never letting up his holy chanting
he kept his eyes skinned for another island.

7.
Brandan's mind was full of islands
he had been born and raised among islands
the Hebrides he knew by heart
the Orkneys and the Faeroes too
the world for him was all islands
and weren't the heavens themselves so made?

he was looking for an island now
but so far North he'd never come
the world here was at an end
here there was only sea and wind

at length he let loose one of his crows
and the crow made straight for the Island of Birds.

8.
Ka! kaya gaya! keeya! keeya!
branta branta! branta branta!
graak! graak! graak!

that island was noisier than a church
all the birds of the ocean had foregathered there

gulls and redshanks and cormorants
kittiwakes, terns and guillemots
geese and gannets and skuas
some perched on pinnacles of rock
others flying wildly about
ah, it was a goodly sight
and music in Brandan's ears

they pulled up the boat on the bit of beach
and turning it into a shelter
settled down for the night.

9.
When Brandan awoke in the morning
he was looking a skua in the eye
and it looked for all the world
like his old teacher, Mernok
away back there in Munster

'Excuse me, Skua', he said, 'can you tell me
how far we are from Paradise?'

the skua gave a sturdy beat of its wings
and stalked silently off
'I thought so', said Brandan.

10.
Ah, it was beautiful, the northern blue
and the clear white curling of the surf!
every mile was a broad blue page of vellum
and Brandan was working out the words

he thought in Latin and he thought in Gaelic
murmuring *'farspag'*, *'in deserto'*, *'muir'*
trying for a freshness never found before

Brandan the voyager would be Brandan the poet
only if he could write a poem
brighter and stronger than all other poems
a poem full of the rough sea and the light

oh, the words for it, the words for a dawning!

to build a boat is good
to sail the faraway seas is good
but to write a poem on which
the minds of men could sail for centuries
that was his ambition now
with a long lifetime behind him.

11.
'*Brandanus laboriosus*' they had called him
when he was a busy abbot of monasteries
true, he had always worked like ten
Brandan the Worker, Brandan the Mariner
he had his reputation, sure
but he'd felt it over there on Iona
when he'd been in talk with that Columba
the one who spouted poetry like a book
that somehow he was out beyond the pale
beyond the pale of the literary folk
lacking their polish, their finesse

Columba the Dove and Brandan the Crow

well, it wasn't polish and finesse he wanted
it was a freshness and a force
and a beauty that they'd never know!

12.
Farther and farther they pulled away
into the white unknown.

Labrador*

1.
Another dawn
out from Greenland
whales bellowing in the icy sea
and the vast sky
resounding with wind

once more I felt that breadth of mind
like being drunk
but this was colder and more clear
than anything
that might come out of a jug
it was what I'd always lived for
what I always will live for
till they throw me
into the trough of the waves
I was used to dance over

there are those who delight
in the storm of swords
and those who make
public speech with words
these are the warriors and the governors
I have preferred other ways
the lonely ways of the sky of sands
the gull path

in all my lonely ongoings
I have thought of many things
I have thought of the earth
in its beginnings
when time was a sequence of cold dawns

and space was full of
the wings of hallucinated birds

I have dreamed of a primal place
a place of rocks, quick streams and emptiness
each morning
the sun rising in the chill sea of the East
and throughout the long day throbbing
above the rocks, above the waters

the earth then was a nameless place
I have been in love with nameless places
now there are too many names
Norway of the blue streams
is rank with names
the Hebrides and even Greenland
names, names, names
and a welter of angry clamourings –
it was time to move farther West

and so another dawn
out from Greenland
and still no other land in sight
only the green waves and the wind
and a vision strong in the mind.

2.
I also named a place
a place of great rocks
and the sun glinting on them
a place filled
with a rush and a flowing of waters
I called it *The Marvellous Shore*

I lived a winter there

it was a time of white silence
I carved a poem on the rocks
in praise of winter and the white silence
among the best runes ever done

men with long eyes and high cheek-bones
came to visit me
I gave them cloth
they gave me skins
there was peace between us

when Spring came
all the streams running with light
and the big river reflecting the sky
I travelled farther South
into a land of forest
I met red men there
dressed like birds

I was aware of a new land
a new world
but I was loathe to name it too soon
simply content to use my senses
feeling my way
step by step into the reality

I was no longer Christian
nor yet had I gone back to Thor
there was something else
calling to me
calling me out
and waiting, perhaps, to be called

something sensual
and yet abstract
something fearsome and yet beautiful

it was beyond me
and yet
more myself than myself

I thought of talks in Norway
the talk of poets and of thinkers
I thought of high talk in the Hebrides

here was no place for Christ or Thor
here the earth worked out its destiny
its destiny of rocks and trees
and sunlight and darkness
worked out its destiny in silence
I tried to learn
the language of that silence
more difficult than the Latin
I learned in Bergen
or the Irish in Dublin.

3.
A whole new field
in which to labour and to think
and with every step I took
I knew a singular health
mind every day more sharp, more clear

I hazarded some more names
(after weighing them carefully every one
trying them out in my mind
and on my tongue):
Great Whale River, Eskimo Point
Indian House Lake, Caribou Pass

but still no name for the whole
I was willing to name the parts

but not the whole

a man needs to fix his knowledge
but he also needs an emptiness
in which to move

I lived and moved
as I had never done before
became a little more than human even
knew a larger identity

the track of caribou in the snow
the flying of wild geese
the red Autumn of the maple tree
bitten by frost
all these became more real to me
more really me
than my very name

I found myself still saying things like
'at one with the spirit of the land'
but there was no 'spirit', none
that was outworn language
and this was a new world
and my mind was, almost, a new mind
there was no such thing as 'spirit'
only the blue tracks in the snow
the flying of the geese
the frost-bitten leaf

religion and philosophy
what I'd learned in the churches and the schools
were all too heavy
for this travelling life
all that remained to me was poetry

but a poetry
as unobtrusive as breathing
a poetry like the wind
and the maple leaf
that I spoke to myself
moving over the land

I am an old man now
an old man very old
I have cut these runes on a rock
to be my testament
perhaps no one will read them
and that is no matter
they will stand on the rock
beside the scratchings of the ice
open to wind and weather.

Logos Amerikanos*

For all those who have tried

1. Port of Santa Maria, 1500

Thinking back eight years
pilot with Columbus

a wide ox-hide spread out before him
ready to make a *mundi carta*
a *pintura de la tierra*
Juan de la Cosa
Basque

Europa... Asia... Africa...
continents chock-a-block with drawings
of men and buildings
then
away West of the marvellous *mare oceanum*
radiant with a great wind-rose of all the universe

a scattering of empty islands.

2. Cape Cod, 1605

The 20th December, it began to snow
and a few blocks of ice
drifted by our habitation

with the coming of Spring, we pursued our discovery

breakers and sandbanks
the sea on all sides flourishing
till we finally made it over
and found a harbour
I called Port-Fortuné

as king's geographer
I drew up a rough little map
bringing in the Kennebec and the Pentagoet
the land of the Etchemins
Cap-aux-Îles and the Beauport
(it will be part of the bigger one
covering the whole territory
from Massachusetts to the Labrador)

all the bays and coasts here
are full of fish and oysters
a thousand-fold shoal of porpoise
glides by the ship every night
and a good place it would be
to found a republic
if only the harbour were a little deeper
and a bit more sure.

3. **Richmond, Virginia, 1728**

Educated in England
I, William Byrd of Westover
had the finest library in the colonies
except maybe for Cotton Mather

I saw to the dividing line
between here and North Carolina
I had ideas for mines
in the Blue Ridge mountains
and for trading with the Indians
(the Georgia people wanted it all their own way)
I thought too we should know a lot more
about the geography of the country
e.g. where the Roanoke rose
and the Potomac

but now at this late hour
it's none of all that state-business I remember
it's that little old opossum
one of our men killed one day at Crooked Creek
what a harmless creature that is
that not only will hardly ever bite
it'll seldom even get out of your road –
take hold of it
all it does is *grin*.

4. **Columbia River, 1804**

Indians here
much afflicted with sore eyes
(all the old folk blind as bats)
dress like those of the coast
except the men
have a craze for brass buttons
that they fix on to sailors' jackets
with no logic I can fathom

(where is America?
where is America going?
where are the United States of being?)

the houses are sometimes sunk
to a depth of three feet
all the posts, doors and beds
adorned with paintings

(I myself Meriwether Lewis
sinking deeper, ever deeper into depression
with no images of any kind
to quicken my mind –
America, oh, America)

stick to the facts:
all are very fond of baths
which they use at all seasons
for health as well as pleasure
every morning
they wash their bodies with urine
(could this make sense?
ladies of Boston, no offence)

the big thing here is *wappatoo*
i.e. arrowhead (*sagittaria sagittifolia*)
which the women gather in ponds
breast-high in the water

they separate the bulb from the root
with their toes
it rises upward out of the mud
to be loaded on canoes

(this is as far
as ethnology goes)

I follow, blind, the trail of all tomorrows.

5. **Mexico City, 1805**

I, Guillaume Dupaix
captain of dragoons, retired
left Mexico City
on the 5th day of January, 1805

my mission:
to seek out monuments of antiquity
dating from before the European conquest

leaving the capital
I travelled East

crossing villages:
Istapahican, Riofrio, Tesurelican, Puebla

where Popocatepec ('smoking mountain')
looms against the empty sky

at Tepeyacan
which in the Mexican language means
'nose of the hill'
I saw the first signs:
on a reddish slab
an eagle
and some glyphs
on a brown-red stone
a head, half-human

two days later
(tough tracks, thick forest)
I was at Teapantepec
'God's house on the hill'
there I found an oratory
in Egyptian style
its four faces
turned to the cardinal points –
on the West face
rose a diagonal path

it is difficult
to give a positive explanation
of such strange forms

likewise of others
found at
Tehuacan, Orizaba, Chapulco
Zongolican

Naranjal, on the banks of White River
Guatusco, Cholula, Atlizco
Quanhquelchula, Cuernavaca
Tetlama, which means 'land of stones'
and Xochicalco, 'house of flowers'

it is said
by an old one in Cuernavaca
these desert places were once all great cities
abandoned by their people
who, tired of rituals and taxes
preferred to fade back into the forest.

6. **Labrador, 1833**

A wooden cabin, windowless
rain dripping through the roof

Audubon (Jean-Jacques)
has just finished painting
the Great Northern Diver
as it cackles over
the cold waters of a lake

the big book was growing

already the first volume
had come out in Edinburgh
a life-work, an epic poem!
the winged dawn of America

as he stowed away yet another sheet
a lone bird cried outside
as if to say, in a wild kind of way
the last word would never be said.

7. San Francisco, 1835

We'd been making for Monterey
but being northward of it
when the wind hauled ahead
we beat a fair way to San Francisco

at a high high point on the S-E
the presidio flaunted its soiled tricolour
behind it, a little harbour
Yerba Buena
close by, the mission of Dolores

no other habitation this side
except a rough board shanty
set up by a man called Richardson
who trades with passing ships and indigenous Indians
who knows (it's the favourite phrase out here)
what this place will look like
a hundred yankee years from now

next to us lay anchored
a very slovenly-looking brig
from Sitka, in Russian America
that had come down South to winter
and take in grain and tallow

despite the rain
that poured and poured for weeks on end
we continued loading hides

though we also played Spanish cards
and sewed together some warm duds
for the long blow back round the Horn.

8. **Arctic Sound, 1923**

The 22nd November, we arrived at Malerisiorfik

the sun is very low
appears above the horizon only at noon
temperature –40, –50

'What brings you here?
are you one of those merchants looking for fox-skins?
– I have come to see you
and to find out who you are.'

the poems here
are not simple hunting songs
or legends of exploits
they call them
'the songs of those who are gone'
they are as old as the world

I went out onto the sea-ice
the seals were blowing in their holes
amazed I
listened to the song of the sea
and the ice's moaning
....
What a joy it is
to feel Summer
come into the Great World
to see the sun
go along its old road
ayaya ya ya

what grief it is
to feel Winter
come into the Great World

to see the moon
go along its old road
ayaya ya ya

to hear these songs
is to hear the sea
battering against an ancient cliff
it is to understand
the first intelligence
of time and the universe.

An Orchestrated Chronicle of the Island

Latitude: 30° 43′ S
Longitude: 55° 13′ E

1.
You leave the Sea of Oman, and come into the Indian Ocean. There, to the south-east of Mogadishu, lies a strung-out archipelago. At the extreme northern tip of this archipelago there is the island in question.

2.
It has, approximately, the shape of a harp. But it changes configuration every year. This year, because the seas have been rougher, or because the general level of the sea is rising, a great part of the North-west, which was an open, sandy expanse, has been covered over by the waters. At this point, the sea keeps pounding and eroding, sculpting out of the land-mass with its rhythmic force ephemeral forms.

3.
Metamorphic weather: the change from the North-west to the south-east monsoon. The sky a soft grey. In it, the sun shining like a moon. Warm wind, thud of waves. Calls of terns and doves. Hovering high in the sky, a silent band of frigates.

4.
Isolation.
To be with the earth, with the earth alone.
Outside all the thought-traps, all the imaginings.
To know a world stripped of fiction, commentary and palaver.
The radical rendezvous.

5.

As they reconnoitre the walls and ceiling of the bungalow throughout the night, the lizards go *tchok-a-tchok, tchok-a-tchok*. They say all they want to say.

6.

The crabs here are darkgreen, blue or rosy-white, with some other little variations. They are thoroughgoing epicureans, adhering strictly to the motto: live hidden, keep quiet. Eight-legged ballerinas, they have two powerful arms, the bigger one for scooping out their holes. As to the disposal of the sand, there are the Pilers and the Spreaders. The former build up conical heaps a foot or so from their holes, so that the beach often looks like an Egypt of pyramids. The others scatter the sand as far as they can in fan-like lines – these close up their holes with a little primped scallop, as neat as any lacework done in a village of the Upper-Loire. I had this classification of Pilers and Spreaders established in my mind when I saw this evening a crab who'd done a pile *and* a fan. Another categorisation gone. The world is always more open than we think.

7.

Big white cumulus galleoning by.

8.

The softbrown bodies, black tail feathers, salt-powdered heads of the noddies. The fine white immaculate brilliance of the albans. The brindled fawnbrown back and short paleblue beak of the dove. All those are in close proximity of the verandah. Some visit frequently: noddies and doves. The alba terns maintain their distance. An occasional visitor is a little Madagascar fody, moulting at this time from flaming crimson back into dusky brown. Further off, towards the north, the sky is filled from time to time with the yammering of the fuliginous ones, turning and turning. And always frigates, solitary, or in a squadron.

9.
I have a little library with me here on the island: Nietzsche, Husserl, Heidegger, those philosophical figures who, I would say, have gone the furthest.

Nietzsche flies about, screaming like a sooty tern, proclaiming the ecstasy of existence.

Husserl sits on his verandah, meditating in a crab-like post-cartesian kind of posture: the phenomenological attitude.

Heidegger is a tortoise. At times, he sticks out his neck and pronounces a few limpid and sensitive sentences about a 'beginning thinking', a 'clearing' philosophy has never heard of, then retreats into his philosophical shell, from which issue complicated sounds of repetitive phraseology.

I read these books when darkness falls.

For the rest of the day, I walk, swim, take notes.

10.
This evening, May 5th, at a secluded part of the island (from a human point of view, the whole island is secluded, but I'm thinking of bird and crab populations), one hundred little hawksbill turtles made their way from a cache up in the bushes down to the sea. The valiant little creatures, an inch and a half long, colour of dry chocolate, scampered and skittered down the sand, sometimes stumbling, sometimes tumbling over themselves, sometimes going off at a tangent, but all making for the light of the sunset and the sea. Pretty soon, a hundred little heads were bobbing in the water. Maybe one or two will survive. Maybe.

11.
Every morning, around 6, I walk round the island, going first north then coming down the eastern shore by Hirondelle Bay and Coco Pass to Point Gros-la-Tête.

This Point ('Big Head') was maybe a spot at which some mariner arrived, finding it difficult to land. I interpret it in my own way as the point at which thought can go no further and has to be relieved by something else.

There's always a band of big crested terns gathered there, nine or so, at the tideline. Scruffy ruffians, these fellows, but with a sturdy elegance. Wild sages of the windy beach. Taoists of the open sea.

12.
I have long been an observer of dawns and auroras. But never I think have I seen an aurora as beautiful as this morning's. The rising sun shot out rays that cut brilliant white paths in the blue. To the south there were two great powerful golden wings. To the north stretched an area of total serenity, with here and there particularly strange and beautiful phenomena: for example, a cluster of little red clouds, like flowers on a flamboyant tree.

13.
A million fuliginous terns came down this evening, May 8th, to nest on the island. That made for a crazy, black-and-white writing in the sky, and a screaming cyclone of noise: in the background, the *whoo-whoo-whoo* of whipping wings; in the foreground, that sustained mass of high-pitched yammering, with here and there an individual call coming through. This band, made up no doubt of several separate bands, will have been flying over the Indian Ocean for a year, always on the wing. When the new brood arrives, they'll move out again. For the moment, they're picking out their spots, preferring places

where the grass has been flattened out or burnt. The Southeast monsoon will bring fish.

14.
Lying out on the beach, like a piece of driftwood.

15.
Kerrak-kerrak-kerrak
Whoo-a-roo, whoo-a-roo
Karakara-karakara
Veedevee
Tria-tria-tria.

The Winter Ceremony*

1.
It's still dark
with big flakes drifting by the window
and the roofs of the outhouses
are all hump-backed
when I switch on the radio:

'Bréhat semaphore calling
this is the national
weather forecast
for the coastal zone
between Cape Fréhel and Lannion Bay
today, 8th January:
very low temperature
under thick cloud
wind from ten to fifteen knots
calm sea
visibility often less
than one mile
with frequent snow'

The whole department of the Côtes-du-Nord
is absolutely snow-bound
it's been snowing on Ushant
for the first time in a century
here at Gwenved
above Lannion Bay
beside the old sanctuary
there's nothing
no noise
only the grey sky, the blue forest
and the long murmur of the sea

Birds cross the sky now and then
gulls and terns
and sea-pies
white, white and black in the white
with an occasional thrush or sparrow
brownly fluttering round the threshold
but mostly there's nothing
just the snow falling
and the hum of the heating plant
here in the study
and the white light
the subdued white light
filtering through the snow-covered window.

2.
'The myth people
were living at Crooked Beach
the house of the Wolves
stoood at the North end of the village
their chief was called
Travelling Wolf...'

It's been snowing for two weeks now
off and on, but over two weeks
when the snow's falling, the horizon's grey
when it isn't falling, the horizon's blue
my eyes have got used to this grey-white-blue
to the wind and the silence
to the isolation
it's going to be none too easy
to pick up again with society...

3.
I've been reading about the Kwakiutl winter ceremony
(Franz Boas's account)
all the dancing
and the storytelling –
but I prefer by far this quieter thing
outside any community

'His name was Lone Wolf
he went round the world
feeling out the lines of the earth
then he holed up in the snow
remembering and listening to the snow'.

4.
Snow over Europe –
that's the title of some thirties' poem
when a red star shone over China
and Left Book Club editions
stood on the shelves of my father's bookcase
a little last snowy peace
before the big show
(some now I hear are nostalgic
for all that noise
for the beliefs and the counter-beliefs
the stances
and the stanzas
about Glory and Humanity and the Future
along with several other themes
which hopefully by this time
have been lifted by the scavengers)

Let's get into the snow out there

Maybe to start off with
singing a little shaman song
something like this:

*There's a bear's head
and a crow's wing
at my door*

*I walk between
blue forest
and white shore*

*nobody knows
what I'm doing here
what I'm looking for*

Are you with me ?

5.
'They went down to Seal Coast
the Wolf People
and the Bear people
and the Crows
they went down to Seal Coast
somebody started beating a drum'

The old heron of the Ile Millau
is wrapped in a blue dream
there's a little band of oystercatchers
freezing on the beach of Pors Mabo

I walk along the shoreline in the snow.

Melville at Arrowhead*

The *White Whale* hadn't made much headway
neither had *Mardi*
as for the *Ambiguities*, it was a total flop
and there was nothing more to be hoped for from
                                       Hawthorne

So he'd retired to the country:
'a supernatural retreat' –
sitting smoking by the chimney
thinking
with always that sense of immensity
and the physical-metaphysical thing
still raging in his brain
(but he'd try and take it easy)

He liked it best
when the snow piled up at Arrowhead
that removed any temptation
to try and go somewhere else
(sure, his wife pestered him a little
he should take this pill or that pill
which would be good for him
and his daughters, well
they were pleasant enough young ladies
but what could they know
went on back of his blue eyes)
sitting there by his chimney
raising smoke-screens
and thinking of impenetrable Japans

Now and then he'd get up
and finger some object

the head of a harpoon maybe, a piece of ivory
that red back of a crab
picked up on the beach at Nuku-Hiva
or else he'd look at some map
its worn red and yellow and blue
and the ocean currents
would be flowing again through his veins
(a white path in a green sea
a quiet lagoon
a spouting of blood
masses of blubber
and Plato's ghost in the fo'c'sle)

What could any citizen
know about his questing?
what could any parlour poet
know about white whales
or unmapped archipelagoes?

Forget them
life wouldn't last long anyway
soon his bones
would be joining the snow in the Berkshires
and the red leaves
in the Autumn woods
never had any regrets

But that brain of his kept working
beyond all simple wisdom:
grappling with uncouth cosmologies
groping along endless blind alleys
as though nothing could ever please it
but the vision of some unheard of poet

'Herman! supper is ready!'

Gauguin in Brittany

What characterized him
was a kind of brutal intellectuality
that he'd demonstrated more than once
in some Parisian café
which was why more tender-hearted artists
hated his guts

he kept hammering one or two points:

'a painting is a plane surface
covered with colour in a certain order'
...
'don't go all out copying nature
art is abstraction'
...
'in art you have to exaggerate
you have to push things right to the limit'

if he left Paris for Brittany
it was to get away from polite society
but also because, out there in the sticks
you could live a lot more cheaply:
bed and board for 60 F a month
at the Gloanec *pension* in Pont-Aven
true, the place was hoatching with painters:
the Scotsman, Donaldson
a bunch of Yankees, Englishmen, Danes and Dutchmen
not to mention all the French –
but there was still plenty of room to move about in

dressed in beret and Breton vest
and in clogs his own hand had sculpted
he liked walking along those rocky paths

that went back to prehistory

'I love this Brittany
I find in it wildness and primitivity
when my clogs echo on the granite ground
I hear the strong dull sound
I want to get onto the canvas'

synthesis, that was it
colour and composition
an energetic simplification

'*la sintaize*, dammit'

not neglecting observation
(e.g. wet sands are definitely red)
but going beyond any simple 'impression'

more and more painters
were listening to what he said

'they're all asking for advice
I put out one clue after another
the buggers use them
to make their work that much better –
which makes me none the richer
but maybe prepares the future'

in search of farther isolation
and in order to get well away
from those who had no conception
of the great 'dreamtime' he was after
but only used bits of his philosophy
to advance their own little career
he left Pont-Aven for the Pouldu
on the banks of the Laïta

where he lodged at the inn of Marie Henry
known locally as 'The Doll'

in no time at all
he and his pupil, Meyer de Haan
had decorated the dining hall
with a wild welter of drawings and phrases
himself he portrayed on a cupboard door
with a halo afloat above his head
in his hands a very supple snake
and a couple of apples at his ear

devils in paradise
(*'Oni soie qui mâle y panse'*)

in the evenings, under the lamp
they drank and smoked and played draughts
or talked 'electrically', about Milton and Carlyle
Hokusai, the Japanese in general

and he continued
clumping about in his clogs
in the depths of blue Brittany
(*'Bonjour, Monsieur Gauguin'*)
painting hay-ricks
red with the red of vision
and potato-fields in flower
and archetypal women
sailing on a ghost ship
into stranger territories

the eye
plunging down into realities
the brain working out that difficult synthesis

'composition... distant creation'

less and less understood
by the boulevard critics over in Paris

in his own mind
striving for ever greater clarity
in this Brittany
with its energy and melancholy
its immemoriality

art, he said, must rise above history.

The Chaoticist Manifesto*

Wave, wind, wing
         plunges
  veers
    play and display
       idea-energies
blue, yellow, white
         the light
     changes
    no knowledge, Mister
     only the being there
   outside
     what you were
    a space
        full of events
  originary practice
     what?
       words without language
         fragmentary syntax
          and yet coherence
      chaos-poem
    this
        that is coming
      Ereignis
        hah!
watch, listen
       white wing
    red roof
   the writing, the thing
     the thing seen, heard
    the thing thought
      raised

        into what
is not metaphysics
            but *claritas*
le bel aujourd'hui
              they're all here
        the thinkers
           those of the *Anfang*
writhing in the wrack
           wheeling in the light
blowing in the wind
           the gathering
      colloque de la côte
towards the plural poem
        chorus
              coruscations
      (where's the Chinaman?
            up there on the hill
running helter-skelter down to the sea
            fengshui)
this is today
      raised out of history
          the pencil
has been sharpened
              the eye
      has been cleaned
the hand confirmed
      no remains
      economy of presence
here now this
      worked out space
          no scheming
      anarchic
            and yet archaic

             (archaic anarchy –
        the most beautiful paradox)
                              Pelagius
          steps out of a hollybush
                       bright!
                Erigena
           walks quiet along the shore
                     sunt lumina
                the mind
                          is inspired
             the landscape
                     enlightened
                the mindscape
             exists
                         (no reason no anguish)
                who what
        without why
             and the questioning
                  fresh
          as the cry
     of the gull on the headland
                        keeya! keeya!
       keeya! keeya!
              here at the sea's edge
     laughing
          laughing a new laugh
               (quotations, quotations
             at home in this topography
                   beyond the nations)
                       whiteness
        is what it means
                 but a whiteness written
     like birch bark

like wave crest
      with lines and with sound
  original
(no ideal, no model)
          eventual
     nothing is absent
  and this body-mind
says it all
      all the ways
lead to here
     have lead to here
  the sky has broken
   and the earth
     sea-washed
    is all diamond.

First Colloquium of the Gull Academy[*]

It was the month of August, on the Breton coast

Whitman was there, at least his ghost
so was Milton, with his *Paradise Lost*

Valéry was there with his ultimate theme
and Bachelard, with the anagogic dream

Mr Rimbaud made the welcome, all in rhyme
the gulls applauded, naturally, all the time.

1.

At the opening session
Mr Wallace Stevens, Jr
director of cosmopoetic studies
at the Renaissance College of Pennsylvania
gave a florid discourse entitled
'From Florence to Florida'
which was followed in the afternoon
by a Reichian lecture on cosmic euphoria
after which
Brigitte served a dish of Lannion lobster.

2.

Another summer day, and low tide
with gulls wailing in the rippled mud

Mr Olson gave a talk on Sumer
the brilliant incoherence of which left the listeners
gasping but glad

the afternoon was devoted
to a meditative walk along the shore
with the Minister of the Environment

who had come from Paris
especially for the occasion
(he had never seen the sea).

3.

This evening
(red sun in the pines)
Mr Yasunari from Yokohama
gave a talk on the floating life
illustrated with exquisite slides
and rare music tapes

at midnight, on the white sands
under the full moon
girls from the Japanese embassy
served warm saké.

4.

'Philosophy and oceanography'
was the subject developed
this morning at 10
by Cpt Whistler of Cape Cod
M. A. (Boston), Ph. D. (Bordeaux)
who quoted Melville, John Donne
Aristotle and the Talmud
(poised
on the table before him
the speaker had a sextant
and charts were pinned exactly on the walls
all round the room)

at lunch
Brigitte served clam chowder
with a glass of rum.

5.

For two hours this afternoon
Professor Dorakis from Thessaloniki
discoursed on the myth of Atlantis
his thesis is
it would have been
(much inflated later by Plato)
an island called Thera
a volcano
imploding

but only the octopuses
really know
and they're not telling.

6.

At 10 this morning
Mr Jean Giono
gave an illustrated lecture
on Manosque-les-Plateaux

he spoke of the wind
and of the light
and of the *descobridores*
who move on ahead of the tribe
when the gipsies
in a long, straggling, colourful line
go down to the sea

at noon
Brigitte served black olives
with a fine white wine.

7.

This evening Mr Ivan Donskoï
of the Russo-Chinese Academy
spoke on meteorites
the one that fell in Alsace
in 1492
the one found near Krasnoïarsk
on the right bank of the Ienissei
in 1749

'stones from the skies'
said, and said again
the peasants and the nomads

'nonsense, nonsense'
said the men of science

'long', said Donskoï, 'is the road of intelligence.'

8.

The Saturday morning lecture
was given by Mr Chou En Lai
from Shanghai
subject: taoist economy

lunch consisted of rice and tea

after which Mr Sun Yat Sen
from the island of Taiwan
gave readings from Li Po
'a gull
lost between earth and heaven'

the gulls, gliding by
were obviously in ecstasy.

9.

Scheduled to speak on
the phenomenology of snow
Mr Merleau-Ponty
just back from Chicoutimi
at the last minute
changed his theme
to one he thought more appropriate
to this morning's climate
'the aesthetics of rain'

the snow lecture has been retained
for a future winter session
to be held in the Pyrenees.

Letter from the Isles of America*

'Do you know Macouba?'

1. *Manoir de Beauregard*

Lying on the
mahogany-pillared bed

reading Labat's *Journey
to the Isles of America*

while the tropical rain
pours down, pours down
over flame-tree, devil-bell, hibiscus

and the frogs raise their evening chorus.

2. *Salines, in the silence*

A grove of curved palms

light wind
swaying the fronds
time here is before
ideas were found

and space wants no sharp lines.

3. *Daybreak on the Caravelle*

The outboardmotor skiffs
have skimmed their white way
to the fishing grounds

lights go out one by one
from the houses in Tartane

now watch the magnificent frigates

as they wheel, swoop and wheel
in the bluebright morning.

4. *In the restaurant at St Pierre*

After a plate
of lentils and rice

gazing through the window
at the diamonding sea

while the old stones of St Pierre
sleep in the sun

and the servant-girl
seems not to know
how beautiful she looks.

5. *Carbet*

Here is where he really learned colour

had come from the Panama
tired out, sick

but he painted
he and Laval

they painted, drank rum
talked
painted, talked
drank rum

five months later, went home

richer by a dream.

6. *Animal kingdom*

The mongoose

noses out, has a keek
then streaks back into the bush

the lizard
head raised, all attention
is a little green yogin.

7. *In the mangrove swamp*

Root breeding root

only a snake
could find his road
hereabout

Euclid, in this place
would go mad
and Aristotle
take to the bottle

but wait
it'll all work out.

8. *Mt Pelée*

There it rises
incredibly clear

like some serene Fuji
in the after-storm air.

9. *Fort-de-France, dusk*

Red hair, dark skin
a man dances wildly on the Savane
while his friends look on
laughing, clapping

Hôtel Lafayette, Hôtel Malmaison

the swashbuckling statue
of the founding father
fades away in the night

what bird has loosed its cry
in the emptiness of the bay?

Elements of the American River System

An initial lesson in geopoetics at Montreal

In this land of mighty waters

all those lakes
that make for the great Canadian Sea

and the rivers:

the St Louis
the Iroquois
the St Lawrence

the Hudson –
flowing broadly down to Angoulême
(now called New York)

the Red and the Mackenzie
the Delaware, the Potomac, the Susquehanna
the Oregon
rapid, snagged, cataractic

and the amazing Mississippi-Missouri

to the West, the Rockies
to the East, the Alleghanies
down to the Gulf of Mexico
in regular curves
(so regular
the Indians measured journeys by the bends)

shady bayous
L'Anse aux Huîtres
the Natchez marshes

mud and driftwood

deep currents
cotton and sugar on the levees

Tell me the Delta
tell me when the sun goes down
tell me the Delta
tell me when the sun goes down...

some other time
we'll talk about the Plata
(its clayey waters still seen
two hundred miles way out in the ocean)

and the Rio Negro
and the Amazonas

that goes West, all force
then South, all form
then back, so strangely, to its source.

The Northern Archives

1. **Shaman talk**

I share the spirit of earth and water
with the hunter and the fisherman

with the hunter
I share duck, hare and deer

with the fisherman
I share cod, seal and whale

but night and mist
the blue sky, the dawn stillness
all the beauty of the elements

these I share with no one.

2. **Praise of the Great Land**

Qajaliurvik
is the place to make a kayak

over by Ikkarvajuq
we wait for seal

it's at Qullibajarniavik
that we find the stone
just right for lamps

at Qilalukkisiivik
we keep our eyes skinned for whale

towards Assaasijuuq
we creep after caribou

at Qamutissait
we gather in the wood

we need for sleds

but some places there are
whose name I will not say

what we do there
is just look around at the great land
hour after hour.

3. Angakok's Letter to the Future

I'm sending you a map of the coast

maybe you'll hear
the rushing of the rivers
and the moaning of the wind over the snow

maybe you'll see the seals
the bears and the wolves

the missionaries make me laugh
it's all too clear from their stories
they don't understand a thing

as for me
I've got no holy name
and my soul is hairy as hell

here's some Northern air for you

and along with my words
I send you eight drum-notes

ayaya!

In the Nachvak Night

Here on the Labrador
in the twilight watching countless birds
settled and asleep
only a few still on the wing
that passing flight of Sabine gulls

is this a death ?
or the prelude to another life?

the question is all too heavy
breenges
into the rippling silence
better simply to wait
taking pleasure in the twilight

tongues of water
tongues of water from the sea of ice
running up the bays and fjords
lapping against the archaean rocks
will say the poem beyond the questioning

the birds are asleep
geese, duck, brant, teal, plover
all are asleep
as though this land were one great sanctuary
a place to rest
on the long trail of the migrations

a place to rest

here in the stillness
halfway between the Old World and the New
moving in deeper
ever deeper

into a world
that is neither old nor new

a world
neither old nor new
on the bird path
feeling it out

......

dawn comes
with the cry of the wild goose.

The Virgins

1.
On Champlain's map
(one of the earliest, if not the first)
a scattering of rough black dots...

2.
This Summer evening
from the tower where I'm standing
I gaze over a wilderness
of cactus, lantana, balsam, logwood
and a chaos of granite boulders

strung out on the skyline
eight other islands
in differing shades of grey.

3.
Devils Bay, 6 a.m.

blue crabs skittering over grey rock
then a congregation of laughing gulls

underwater
a fluttering cloud of tangs
a silent armada of barjacks

a blacktip shark.

4.
That rocky islet there
where the sea's apocalyptical
and the stone comes straight out of hell
is called Fallen Jerusalem.

5.

Other names are:
Salt, Guana, Ginger
Norman, Peter
Tortola, Virgin Gorda
The Dogs
Camanoe
Jost Van Dyke

old Indian words
resources
passing skippers
religious references
vague resemblances

(anyway
back of all the names
what matters).

6.

Chasms and dark abysses

opening out on to
gardens of delight.

7.

Anegada
with its reefs of high coralheads
is the place of shipwrecks

on its nihilistic sands
a pond of flamingos.

8.
All the long afternoon
over the wilderness
the shrill cries of kestrels.

9.
In the late July
heavy showers
go hissing and drumming their way
across Sir Francis Drake's Channel
in those days
the whole seascape
is arched with rainbows.

10.
Evening coming on

after roaming and grazing
all day where they can

the sleek brown cattle of the island
are lying themselves down.

11.
A tropical storm
baptised Apollo

born in a depression
off the Cape Verde isles

travelling up over the Atlantic
at nineteen miles an hour

gathering strength
calling in all-wandering clouds

heading North
veering West

may hit this island
with hurricane force
on the night of August 3rd.

12.

Around the midnight

a blue wind
howling about a house of glass.

On the Florida Keys

North of Cancer
but tropical territory

on a spit of low scrubland
a wooden cabin

piled on shelves
wormeaten, sand-dry volumes
from the State Department of Conservation:
Geology of Florida
Scenery of the Peninsula
Louis Agassiz on the Reef

beyond the scrub
a shore of greywhite mud
with scattered coral

palmettos, still or slowly moving, on the skyline

on the shore:
the red zone
the black zone
the white zone

fleshy grasses
lichens and moss-weeds
purple-clawed hermits
fastrunning yellowgrey ghosts

barnacles, limpets, whelks
mussels, urchins, anemones
small dark-edged oysters

there is the place I haunt
day after day after day

this afternoon, with a high wind blowing
the sea is the colour of nothing.

Finisterra* *or* The Logic of Lannion Bay

It's in the shape of the headlands
it's in the way the wave
breaks along the shoreline
(with a slow motion *shpoof* against the rocks)
it's in the variant light
it's in the crystal clear silence of this April morning

up at Yaudet
which was Roman ground
before it yielded
to the syntax of Christianity
you can watch the Léguer
(which recalls the Loire
as well as all other Ligurian waters)
running down to its estuary
in brilliant bluegreen ripples

thereafter
to walk along the coastal path
from, say, Goaslagorn valley
to the beach of Pors Mabo
is to move between foam and flourish
wondering what whiteness
you'll ever be able to add to *those* whitenesses

the points one has in mind
are Dourven
(off it, the wreck of the *Azalea*)
Bihit
hiding to view the isle of Milo
(to whom Brandan may have paid a friendly visit)
and way far off
lost in the light and spray

the land's end, Roscoff

heather, thorn and pine
gorse and whin
rush down
to curving sandy beaches
and it's a large arc of land
indicating the Atlantic
lies extended before you

years ago, I remember
when first I came here
sitting with my back to a pine
above Pors Mabo
reading Pyrrho
in Estienne's XVIth century version:
'Is this work serious
or is it just full of noise?
– I'll think it over.
– What's it all about?
– I don't get the drift of your question.
– What have you defined?
– I never define.
– What do you do, then?
– I just keep looking.'

looking at this place
looking into this place
and at the same time
into the circuits of my mind
in Summer dawns
in golden Autumn evenings
in chill Winter mists
something like those old taoists

who founded the Academy of Gulls
(a bird and an eye, a bird and an eye:
ideogram for monastery)
an academy without walls
active contemplation: no ideals, no idols
and no over-hasty
over-personal, over-poetical projections
rather long-ranging recognitions
in space and in time

as one who has studied
the grammar of granite
I have walked here
as one who would equate
landscape with mindscape
I have walked here
as one who loves
the ways and the waves of silence
I have walked here

who knows
maybe in years to come
some time after the aftermath
a curious tourist from outer space
will walk along this selfsame path
and be aware of my ghost:
still looking out at the lines
still looking into the light.

The Domain of Gwenved

1.
Reading Erigena
in the Atlantic super-express:
vistas of periphyseonic space.

2.
Breton land:
terns and tridactyls
manoeuvring in the wind.

3.
Hearing seamews
but when I raised my head
only the moon.

4.
Around this workroom
listen to it prowling
the wind of the earth.

5.
This early snow
makes you want to read
only words full of silence.

6.
In the white mist
above Landrellec
the song of the cuckoo.

7.
Ah, those Spring days
on the Eastern shores
on the Western shores.

8.
A night in June
at the marsh's edge
the call of the curlew.

Low Tide at Landrellec

1.
Tide still high

gulls immaculate
on lofty ledges

ocean quiet.

2.
Slowly very slowly
the sea quits the rocks

leaving a line
of ancient weeds

where a sharp-eyed crow
forages for goodies.

3.
Sands now laid bare
some smooth, some rippled

the sea a blue glitter in the distance
long afternoon silence

broken by gull-cries.

4.
Among the far rocks
weird marine growth

a baroque beauty:

that rash of rough barnacles

limpets
close as Chinese

over there
thickblueblack
a layer of mussels

swaying patches of Poseidon grass.

5.
In this still pool

among yellow-green sponge
pink hydroids
and the blue of Irish moss

sidling crabs
feel out their paths.

6.
In this other
moon-jellies

the green flesh
crowns of anemones

northern starfish.

7.
That crab (a Jonas?)
wedged in a handy crevice

antennae waving

waiting.

8.
Hearing the tide
now swirling back in

breaking white here and there
on the coastline

sun going down
cold gold.

Lament for McManus

It's a blue diamond evening over Lannion Bay
the sea is whispering up against the shore
and the gulls are yelling homewards

the news came through this afternoon
that you died this April morning
of the cancer that after lingering
had speeded up and reduced you
almost to a skeleton

as I walked along the Goaslagorn valley
 the air was full of bird notes
some close some far
like some unfinished symphony

I was remembering
the last time we walked together
that was at Cramond, Edinburgh
along the banks of the Almond River
talking about Duncan Ban Macintyre
and about the name he gave to the Lowlands
the *Machair Alba*

when suddenly we saw a heron
standing still and so absolutely attentive
in the midst of the rippling water

the way the mind can be at its best
as you well knew, McManus
son of the celto-galatian West
always looking for the words and the music
to say that highness

it's the flowers of the machair here

whin flowers and blackthorn bloom
with sprigs of purpurine heather
I'm scattering over your grave, McManus
over by Mortonhall
at the end of your fight

but it's thinking of what your mind was after
that I'm looking at that first star
shining away up there to the North
in the clear erigenian light.

The Poetics of Rain

'What are you doing now?', he said
'I'm studying rain'

reading
(as I listen to it falling
over the rock and soil and sand
of this autumnal terrain)
Meunier's *Geological History of Rain*
Curtis's *Analysis of the Causes of Rainfall*
and *Rain and Wind in Spain*
by Mor de Fuentes

what better place than this
the sea-province of the West
for such an enterprise

Curtis distinguishes three types of rain:
convective
orographic
cyclonic

remembering rain over Martinique
drum-drum-drumming on banana leaves
at the Manoir de Beauregard
(bullfrogs buddha-like on the floor)

or in monsoon weather
out there in the Seychelles
hissing over
that forgotten little atoll

rain in a Pyrenean valley
the Aspe or the Ossau
the smell of wood-fire

the drenched grey heights
the rushing torrents

rain on the wrack-strewn shore
of a Scottish village

rain beating on a skylight window
on Park Avenue, Glasgow
or in Paris
on the Boulevard Richard-Lenoir

and how many rainy excursions
across this land of stones
throughout the year...

in the hot stench
of the planet's beginning
it was rain made it possible to breathe

even nowadays
after its passage through some stifled city
the air can suddenly smell of iodine

sweeping the atmosphere
the rain gathers together
all kinds of heterogeneous matter

there have been red rains
yellow rains
as well as white, black and grey rains:
in 1897
it rained salt water in Utah

slowly but surely also
rain writes the earth:
watch it furrowing the soil out there
gouging little ravines –

so it has done with many a mountain
many a glen

take a sinuous river like the Seine
and consider all its divagations
what delicate, determined action
created those curves –
always aided and abetted
for the finishing touches
by the rain

rain works in multiple ways

if snails can turn marble into sponge
so can the rain

its influence is all-pervasive

the nature of this wild water
results in all kinds of strange phenomena

Lenier in his *Estuary of the Seine*
says when the cliffs crumbled
at La Hève, Normandy, in 1800
there was a phosphorescent gleaming
from the fissures
(the rain had been secretly at work again)

no poetics of the planet
can neglect the workings of rain

the movement and the music of rain.

Late August on the Coast*

Prologue
Ah, the breathtaking beauty of this late August, now the
summer people are gone, and the beaches silent again –
   great mists rising up over the sea
   and moving inland
   along the little valleys
   (all morning it's a misty world
   a quiet *Niflheim*)
   but by early afternoon
   the mist bank breaks
   now here, now there
   revealing bluegleaming stretches of water
   a piney wood
   a red fern moor
   a stony village...

Rain, tea and a butterfly
   Eight o'clock
   grey sky and a quiet rain
   I want to enjoy (and maybe ingeniously employ)
   long hours of this
   so I've unplugged the telephone
   (ah, this delicious sensation
   of total isolation – I just hope
   no one will turn up spontaneously
   to ask me if I believe in God
   or invite me to come and turn tables
   or tell me about their family squabbles...)
   I look around
   at a few things I have on the wall:
   a 19th century print of a blue rorqual

(1/72 natural size)
stranded on a misty, rocky shore,
a leaf from a zoological album
showing a grey-backed seal
(*pélage moine*
squelette de la tête vu de profil)
and a page out of
Grønlandske Fangere Fortaeller
showing eight fishes of Greenland
from the polar cod, *gadus callarius*
to the sleeping shark, *somniosus microcephalus*
(we whose homeland
is the world
as the sea is to fish
says Dante –
but what's the world?)...
the eye moves on to
a Japanese print
'Kambara: snow at night'
and to another
'Sunset on a snowy day at Uchikawa'...
I go make some tea
the red earthenware pot
is now set at my elbow
I'll lie out there on the bed
with the Tunisian blanket
(Avicenna, ah, Avicenna)
drink the tea while it's hot
and watch the rain
the quiet-falling rain
through the philosophical window:
there's a butterfly there
some kind of Admiral

(I'm more than a little vague about admirals)
maybe it's old Chuang-tzu
come out of the tea pot
(why not, after all?)
to talk with me about the tao:
OK, butterfly, what's the tao?
(like, at least grammatically
what's the time?)
flutter flutter, a red flutter-flutter
(I feel my pulse:
the answer to an existential question
can never be mathematical) –
there's Reich and Heidegger walking by...
rain and tea and a butterfly:
do I have here the makings
of a fiction supreme?
will this rainy day
at August's end
give me a new look into reality
or a wonderful waking dream?
I go downstairs
read a page or two of Melville
a page or two of Thoreau
a page or two of *The Oregon Trail*
(I intend some day
to write a series of lectures
on 'American space' and the question of the real
that'll make David Herbert Lawrence and the rest
sound like *Paris-Match* or the *Reader's Digest*)...
the butterfly's still fluttering at the window
I pour tea in the cup again
and lie there listening to the quiet rain.

Epistle to the Birds of this Coast
>You gulls who know this coast
>from the Aber Wrac'h to the Seven Islands
>you of the red-tipped beaks
>you sterns and kittiwakes
>you oyster-catchers
>you band of ghostly herons
>still holding out on the Île Millau
>(I see you in the evening
>over the pine wood
>grey-blue in the blue)
>this is just to say
>I'm glad and grateful that you're there
>because if you weren't
>if you were all gone
>that would mean the others had won
>the advancing ones
>the constructive ones
>with their crazy beliefs and their lousy ideologies
>their oil-slicks and their nuclear garbage
>their noises and their nuisances
>(they don't know how to walk the coast
>they have to have all kinds of
>games and animations
>they don't even know what they've lost) –
>so
>please keep on using the sky
>as you know how
>riding the wind
>with your eyes wide open
>tracing out the shoreline
>(along with something else it's harder to define)
>and throw out a cry or two now and then

for those of us down here who care
that'll be a kind of reminder
(to accompany the signs
we read silent in the stone):
way beyond the heart's house
right into the bone.

The Nameless Archipelago
Out there
nameless
sometimes in certain lights
I think I have it
(that last glance over the coast rocks
in the gathering evening...
or in the white mist of early morning)
but there's no exactitude
(I'm not content to be a mystic)
at other times I get exactness
but I feel it as fragment
(like picking up a stone
with no sense of geology)
I can sometimes even feel part of it myself
when I'm swimming in the sea
(marine yoga, kind of)
but that's not knowing it
and there's no expression
(I'm not even sure any more what 'knowing' means
and as to expression
I don't just mean poetry
I suppose what I'm after is closer
to a kind of cartography)...
in the map room here
looking at the world of

Dionysius Periegetes
(*Celtae, Scythae, mare cronium*)
the periplum of Pytheas up to Thule
a nautical atlas
(Portugee, early 16th century)
of the North-East Atlantic
(*oceanus britannicus, mare iperboreum*)
Al Sharqi's map of the Mediterranean
a Korean map of China and Japan
and a Blue River itinerary...
sometimes
maybe to make things easier
I imagine this nameless place
as a bird sanctuary
peopled with creatures whose brains
are less complex than mine
so that for them
everything clicks all the time
(it's true that merely to hear
the cry of some gull on the shore
is enough to awaken – *wakan!* –
the old 'metaphysical' desire):
to say it's a sanctuary
is to say it's admirable
but uninhabitable...
how to inhabit (intimately)
a place with no name? –
one would have one's-self
to have no name
but if there are no names
what can one say?

The Music of the Landscape
    Listening in
    (late August morning)
    to the music of the landscape:
    sea-wind
    blowing veil after veil of grey
    up the valley of Goaslagorn
    flights of wailing birds
    over the fields
    young birches
    with scarcely frosted trunks
    rain-whispering
    hoarse ragged firtrees on the skyline...
    along the shore
    (all the islands wrapped in mist
    but the surf outlines them
    with silent thunder)
    a restlessness, a movingness
    a chaos-noisiness:
    unruled masses of sound
    interrupted by sharp cries
    or a wave breaking
    on ice-scored rock
    (no place this for
    sympathies or symphonies
    any kind of easy
    harmonisation:
    the weather is everchanging
    and from Dourven point
    to Ploumanac'h's centred complex
    the topography abrupt) –
    yet there is
    something like a music there

in the grey rain
and the sharp cries
and the wind
that travels the changing skies
there is something
immensely
satisfying to the mind
corresponding
to its highest demand:
admitting no simple equations
and laughing at any solemn questions.

A Short Introduction to White Poetics
    Consider first the Canada Goose
    brown body, whitish breast
    black head, long black neck
    with a white patch from throat to cheek
    bill and legs black
    flies in regular chevron or line formation
    flight note: *aa-honk*
    (that's the one old Whitman heard on Long Island)

    Then there's the Barnacle Goose
    black and white plumage
    white face and forehead
    (in German, it's *Weisswangengans*)
    flight in close ragged packs
    flight note
    a rapidly repeated *gnuk*:
    gnuk gnuk gnuk gnuk gnuk gnuk gnuk
    (like an ecstatic Eskimo)

    Look now at the Brent Goose
    small and dark

black head, neck and breast
brilliant white arse
more sea-going than other geese
feeds along the coast
by day or by night
rapid flight
seldom in formation
irregularly changing flocks
her cry:
a soft, throaty gut-bucket *rronk*

The Red-Breasted Goose
has a combination of
black, white and chestnut plumage
legs and bill blackish
quick and agile, this beauty
seldom flies in regular formation
cry:
a shrill *kee-kwa kee-kwa*
(who, what? who, what?)

The Greylag
pale grey forewings
thick orange bill
lives near the coastline
flies to grazing grounds at dawn
usually in regular formation
cry: *aahng ung-ung*
(like a Chinese poet
exiled in Mongolia)

As to the Bean Goose
she has a dark forewing
and a long black bill

talks a lot less than other geese
just a low, rich, laconic *ung-unk*

The Snow Goose
has a pure white plumage
with blacktipped wings
dark pink bill and legs
(in North America turns blue
a dusky blue-grey)
in Europe you might take her for a swan
or maybe a gannet
till she lets you know abruptly
with one harsh *kaank*
she's all goose

so
there they go
through the wind, the rain, the snow

wild spirits
knowing what they know.

Scotia Deserta

All those kyles, lochs and sounds...

*   *   *

And the gulls at Largs pier:
sitting in that café
at the big window full of wind and light
reading and watching

*   *   *

Thinking back to the ice
watching it move
from the high middle spine
out into the Atlantic

feeling it gouge out lochs
and sculpt craggy pinnacles
and smoothe long beaches

the land emerges
bruised and dazed
in the arctic light

gannets gather on the islands
eagles on the piney hills
cotton grass tosses in the wind

men come
gazing around them
what name shall be given it?
Alba

*   *   *

White beach meditations
mountain contemplations

imprinted on the mind

*   *   *

One left traces of his presence
out there in Bute and the Garvellach Isles
and in Kilbrannan Sound –
the holy voyager, Brandan

Brandan was maybe a believer
but that's neither here nor there
first and foremost
he was a navigator
a figure moving mile by mile
along the headlands
among the islands
tracing a way
between foam and cloud
with an eye to outlines:

Sound of Islay
the Firth of Lorn
Tiree passage
the Sound of Mull
Skerryvore and Barra Head
Loch Alsh, Kyle Rhea
Sound of Raasay

*   *   *

Ah, the clear-sounding words
and a world
opening, opening!

*   *   *

Other figures cross the scene
like this one:

Kentigern they cried him

in the church I attended
around the age of nine
was that stained glass window
showing a man
with a book in his hand
standing on a seashore
preaching to the gulls

I'd be gazing at the window
and forgetting the sermon
(all about good and evil
with a lot of mangled metaphor
and heavy comparison)
eager to get back out
on to the naked shore
there to walk for hours on end
with a book sometimes in my hand
but never a thought of preaching in my mind

trying to grasp at something
that wanted no godly name
something that took the form
of blue waves and grey rock
and that tasted of salt

*   *   *

A rocky walk
and the smell of kelp
between Fairlie and Largs

Drifting smoke
the glint of autumn leaves
on Loch Lomondside

Ghostly gulls in the greyness
keeya, keeya, keeya, keeya
September at Applecross

Tiree
on a March morning
the kingdom of the wind

Seven islands
in the August sunlight
Islay, Jura, Scarba, Lunga, Luing, Shuna, Seil

*   *   *

Walking the coast
all those kyles, lochs and sounds

sensing the openness
feeling out the lines

order and anarchy
chaos and cosmology

a mental geography

*   *   *

Have you heard Corrievreckan
at the Spring flood
and a westerly blowing?

the roaring's so great
you can hear it twenty miles
along the mainland coast

admiralty charts
show a 9-knot race

to the senses
that do no calculations

but take it all in
it's a rushing white flurry

birthplace
of a wave-and-wind philosophy

*   *   *

Let the images
go bright and fast

and the concepts be extravagant
(wild host to erratic guest)

that's the only way
to say the coast

all the irregular reality
of the rocky sea-washed West

*   *   *

Pelagian discourse
atlantic poetics

from first to last.

Notes

BOOK I

Pelagius – This British monk was born about AD 350, that is, roughly at the same time as St Augustine, and died in 430. Leaving the western island, he travelled first to Rome, then to Africa and the near East. He opposed the Augustinian theory of original sin, saying that nature was a good basis, you just had to work on it. St Augustine's doctrinal system came out victor of the debates: Pelagian theory was refuted and condemned at the Council of Ephesus in 431. But there's a pelagian current running right through European literature, at least underground. It's there in Erigena. It's there in André Breton ('Pelagius, your head erect over all those bended brows' – Ode to Charles Fourier). It's there in this Open World book. Jerome was sent on a mission by St Augustine to keep the Pelagians in order. The original Latin from which I translate was this: *Scotorum pultibus praegravatus*. Jerome and Augustine weren't the only ones to be exasperated by the Pelagians. 'Who are those people of the West,' cried a bishop, 'who dare to disagree with the whole world?!'

The Wandering Jew – Among the numerous mediaeval 'books of hours', that tell the course of the year, one of the most beautiful is that of Anne de Bretagne, which dates from the fifteenth century. I like the lines and the colours and the atmosphere of the seasonal miniatures, less fantastic than Bosch, less boisterous than Breugel, but every bit as vigorous. There was a clarity and an edge in those 'dark ages', and the beginnings of 'landscape-mindscape'.

In the Botanic Gardens, Glasgow – No need to present in detail the eigthteenth century master of haiku, Bashô, but I seize the opportunity to quote his warning to poets: 'No matter how perfect your technique, if your feeling isn't natural, if you're cut off from reality, you'll only produce a semblance of the real thing.' If I had to live with only ten books, Bashô's *Narrow Road to the Deep North* (*Oku no Hosomichi*) would probably be one of them. The Tibetan Poppy was introduced into British gardens in 1924, the date also of the first Surrealist Manifesto, which was *not* introduced into British gardens.

What Enid Starkie Didn't Know – Enid Starkie, professor of French literature at Cambridge, biographer of the poet Arthur Rimbaud, was the external examiner at my finals in Glasgow. Eager to ascertain how 'the man with the wind on his heels' had got out of Java in 1876, she consulted assiduously all the British shipping records at Cardiff, seeing no sign of him. This poem is my solution to her problem.

In a Café at Largs – Largs is a small town on the west coast of Scotland. Facing the pier, there used to be a café, with large bay windows, called The Moorings. It was a place I frequented a lot as a student, and later, especially early in the morning when customers were few.

Passing by the University in Glasgow – The phrases in French, respectively from Montaigne, Rabelais and Mallarmé, can be translated so: 'An original and peculiar form', 'fine books full of marrow' and 'the brain drunk with a confusion of light'.

The Ballad of Kali Road – Caledonia Road on the South Side of Glasgow is locally known as Cale Road. From Cale to Kali it only took a phonetical, transcultural, metaphysical hop, step and jump, all the easier to make in that the Indian population of the South Side was strong. This long poem incorporates some 'songs' that were originally published in *The Cold Wind of Dawn* (Jonathan Cape, London, 1966).

On the Border – The meeting with the vultures took place on the Urculu plateau in the Pyrenees.

At the Solstice – In section I, Schiehallion (the sacred hill of the Caledonians) is a mountain in the north of Scotland. The lines in section V are from an old French poem that evokes the ragged-cloaked Wandering Scot of the Middle Ages.

BOOK II

To the Bone – Fairlie is a small village on Scotland's west coast, about three miles from Largs. I spent all my childhood there.

The Eighth Climate – The Greek division of the inhabited world into seven climates: Climate of Egypt, Climate of Ethiopia, and so on, was wellknown in the Middle Ages, notably from Pliny's *Natural History*. Pliny's seventh climate, the most northerly, stops at Venice. He indicates three others, but only in a very sketchy fashion. A thirteenth-century map done by John of Wallingford at the abbey of St Alban's has an eighth climate that includes Anglia, Hibernia and Scotia, placing Scotland practically at the North Pole.

The Book at Lismore – The Book of the Dean of Lismore, a manuscript put together by James and Duncan MacGregor in the early sixteenth century, is the most ancient collection known of Scottish Gaelic poetry. As to Finn (finn = white), as in *Finnegans Wake*, he is one of the central figures in the whole Celtic tradition. He probably goes back to the white shamanism of neolithic deer-cults. But in historical times (the beginning of the Christian era), the Companions of Finn (the Fianna) were outlaws, out to defend the undefended. To be a Companion, you had to renounce all clan and family ties, be physically fit (able to run fast and jump long), and know by heart the twelve books of poetry.

For MacDiarmid – Scottish poet (1892–1978), the leader of what was called the 'Scottish Renaissance'. The reference in the last line is to his long poem 'Diamond Body', but also, beyond it, to the whole 'diamond body' context. See the note below to *Handbook for the Diamond Country*.

McTaggart – William McTaggart, Scottish painter (1835–1910). McTaggart in his evolution moved away from genre and narrative to landscapes made up of pure light and primal phenomena. It was the Scottish development of a painting that had begun in France, in the forest of Fontainebleau, at Barbizon, before going to Brittany.

Pool Poem for MacCaig – Norman MacCaig, Scottish poet (1910–1996), who loved fishing in the rivers and lochs of the North-West. Duncan Ban and Rob Dunn: eighteenth century Scottish Gaelic poets.

Dunbar – A little town on the east coast of Scotland, south of Edinburgh. Dunbar was the birthplace of the man, John Muir (1838–1914), who was to be the great defender of wilderness in North America. The light referred to is that of the Bass Rock.

Three American Beers – That was some night. A great sensation of space. Euramerasian ecstasy. The beers are only metaphor. The Henry in question is of course Henry Thoreau, in his book, *The

Maine Woods, the first section of which is devoted to his approach to what he writes as Ktaadn. That phrase I quote of his is a criticism of the restricted space of Common Sense philosophy. I'm also making philosophical fun here of a certain brew of metaphysical ponderousness.

Culross – Culross is an old Scots town lying north-east of the Firth of Forth. Among its vestiges of sixteenth-century Scottish architecture is a two-storey house called The Study.

Report to Erigena – John Scot Erigena left Ireland (it's the ninth century), no doubt because of the Viking invasions. He sought refuge in France, at the court of Charles the Bald, where he studied the work of Denys the Areopagite before plunging into his own work on *The Divisions of Nature*. The authorities of the time accused him of contravening both discipline and doctrine (his was a wild, bright mind), and his philosophy was considered as belonging to the pelagian heresy. He was condemned by the Church, which has a long memory, in 1225, four centuries after his death in 877. His phrase *sunt lumina* ('there are lights') refers to those 'divine apparitions comprehensible to intellectual natures' that are part integral of his philosophy. I take Erigena to be one of the prime examples of the Celtic intellectual, and look for signs of that tradition today, the tradition of the *Scotus vagans*, those whom Renan (in his *Poetry of the Celtic Races*) called 'teachers in grammar and literature to all the west', 'studious philologists and bold philosophers'. In Frederick Artz's book *The Mind of the Middle Ages*, Erigena is presented as the greatest figure of the Carolingian renaissance and one of the loneliest minds in the history of Western thought.

Reading Marpa in the Blue Mountains – Marpa, called 'the Translator', lived and worked in Tibet. He was one of the founders of 'the White Line' that included Tilopa, Naropa and Milarepa. The 'Blue Mountains' are the Cairngorms, but if I designate them so, it was because I was thinking also of the Chinese buddhist text, *The Blue Cliff Records*, an eleventh century collection of koans indicating the path to enlightenment.

Sesshu – The Japanese painter Sesshu (1420–1506) did in painting what Bashô did in writing. As Su Tung-p'o said: 'Poetry and painting aim at one and the same thing: an effortless skill and an unmixed freshness.'

Kenkô – Urabe Kaneyoshi, who took as his monk's name Kenkô, which is the Chinese pronunciation of the two characters *kane* and *yoshi*, was born in 1283. After occupying a minor official position at the imperial court in Kyoto, where he was highly esteemed as scholar and poet, he broke with wordly affairs around the age of thirty-five and retired to the hills. He set up various hermitages, first on Mt Hiei, later at Yoshida, and finally at the Ninna-ji temple, west of Kyoto. So, there was the hermit's life, but there was also the life of the traveller (he made trips to the Kiso region, Lake Biwa, Kôbe...), and he continued his researches into Chinese and Japanese culture, notably in the library at Kanazawa. As poet, he belonged to the Mikohidari school, founded by Fujiwara Shunzei (1114–1204), and developed by his son Teika, the man who compiled the famous *Hundred Poems* anthology.

Round North Again – In Ch'an Buddhism, the phrase 'going back home' means the dissolution of the personal ego, the experience of emptiness, the discovery of one's 'original face'.

A Short Lesson in Gaelic Grammar – I have no claim, except in a passing way, to the Gaelic, but I've done with Gaelic what I've done with several other languages: I've read everything I could find in translation, and I dip into grammars, dictionaries, and annotated original texts now and then. The idea is to awaken things latent in myself rather than actually learn the language. Maybe essential characteristics stay longer in the bones than on the tongue, maybe you can push things farther by not settling in any one tradition. To come to that white stone, in a poem of the Gaelic poet Iain Lom (seventeenth century) a woman is compared to a white pebble. And in a Scots poem by William Soutar (early twentieth century), the poet is visited at night by a woman with fresh lips and little round breasts ('I kent her by her caller lips, and her briests sae sma' and roun'). There's a white stone also at the centre of Chinese logic: see Chapter 5 of the *Kong-souen Long*. In other words, this little linguistic poem is carrying erotic logic.

Beinn Airidh Charr – This is a mountain in Wester Ross, overlooking lovely Loch Maree.

A High Blue Day on Scalpay – Scalpay is an island in the Outer Hebrides.

On Rannoch Moor – This wild plateau in Northern Scotland has always had an attraction for me. I keep going back to it.

Early Morning Light on Loch Sunart – The Gaelic lines quoted are from a poem by Duncan ban MacIntyre (1724–1812). The poem is entitled *Oran Ghlinn Urchaidh*, 'Ode to Glen Orchy', and Englished, the lines say this 'Fresh water salmon were found there, heading up every stream, and moorland birds in multitudes.'

Alba – I'm using 'Alba' here as the old name for Scotland ('the land of the white heights'), but also with reference to the Provençal 'dawn–song'.

Winter Letter from the Mountain – In his *Vajrayana* ('diamond vehicle') *Meditations*, C. M. Chen has this: 'In the highest tantra, wherever one happens to be, that is the mandala, whatever syllables one utters, these are the mantric syllables.' It's good to keep this in mind when you hear some people who are 'into the East' merely mouthing exotic formulae. The thing is, to get to the top of the mountain – and keep climbing. Into clear air.

Mountain and Glacier World – Maurice Blanchot talks of 'that place... that farthermost region we can designate only in negative terms as a nothingness, but a nothingness which is also the veil of being'. There was no real temptation of suicide here. All I wanted to do was 'blow my mind', in order to get out of mental cinema into the white.

Late December by the Sound of Jura – On the west coast of Scotland, you have as anarchic a cluster of islands as in Greece. The heights of Jura, called The Paps, put a kind of elemental female energy in the air. If you put that energy beside the idea of 'sound' (as in the Sound of Jura), you maybe have the prelude to a poetics. In a letter Victor Segalen, the Franco-Breton poet, wrote after a talk he had had on his way back from China with the Russian sinologist Alexeiev concerning the relationship between poetry and Taoism, I read this, years after writing the poem: 'Inspiration is a sound of the Tao, very rare, and wellnigh inaudible ... The ideal of poetry is a deep intuition that accumulates in silence and shows itself with hardly a word being pronounced.' As to Alexeiev himself, here's what he says about taoist poetic intuition in his little book on Chinese literature. 'A veil of snow on a little island, that is the symbol of pure inspiration. Its whiteness in the moonlight leads to a sense of integral unity.' And, here, in the same area, is

Jacques Maritain speaking of certain Chinese poems: 'Such poems are very condensed and concentrated, expression is reduced to the essential, allusive touches take the place of any kind of rhetorical or discursive development. But however clear these poems be, however explicit and intelligible, their meaning is somehow unlimited, or, we might say: open.' I'm no Thomist, but Maritain's *Creative Intuition in Art and Poetry* (1954) was my start into the field of aesthetics.

Theory – The word 'theory' as title of this poem may seem totally out of place. A hard-minded epistemologist will say (1) that a theory is based on observation and experience, (2) that it can be refuted or verified, (3) that its function is to render coherent and conceptualize data hitherto isolated and unexplained. Little of that in this poem. But theories, like methodologies, can be a block on thought, especially when only a certain *type* of theory, a certain *type* of methodology is entertained. Maybe this poem goes back to a more primordial sense of theory, the one still present in Aristotle when he says that life spent in theory is a kind of divine life, ontologically extraordinary. The original meaning of the word is 'a procession of beautiful ideas'. In *The Illuminations*, Rimbaud speaks of 'secret places lit up by the entry of theories'.

Late Summer Journey – The geographical location here is the archipelago of the Outer Hebrides.

Last Page of a Notebook – The Japanese words, whose source is the text known as *The Gateless Gate*, are a definition of absolute reality 'Neither mind, neither Buddha, nor a thing.' Kyle of Tongue is a stretch of water in the far north of Scotland.

BOOK III

Walking the Coast

Wave II – The quotation is from a modern Gaelic poem, *A' Chorra – Gritheach* ('The heron') by Sorley Maclean (1911–1996). It is translated in the lines that follow.

Wave III – The scattering of words at the beginning of this section are Scottish dialect names for the gull. The little Gaelic phrase at the end, which I may have lifted from a text or which I may have made up (my Gaelic went to that) is Englished in the final line.

Wave IV – The phrase in Welsh is translated in the lines that follow.

Wave XVIII – The reference is to the Austrian painter, Oskar Kokoschka (1886–1980). Expressionist painting meant a lot to me when I lived in Glasgow. It was saying two things: that art is more than constructivist formulae, and that the world is more than a jumble of symbols.

Wave XX – Hakuyu (literally, 'White Obscurity') was born in 1646. He lived a hermit's life in the Kitashirakawa mountains. That's where Hakuin Zenji (he tells the story in his *Night Talk on a Boat*), who had got himself ill owing to an over-zealous practice of meditation, went to visit him in hope of a cure. Hakuyu told him to go away and cure himself.

Wave XXIV – The Norwegian painter Eduard Munch (1863–1944) was another painter whose work was close to me in Glasgow, less maybe *The Cry* than *White Night*. The lines I quote are fragments of a conversation that took place at Munch's house at Skoyen, near Oslo, in 1937.

Wave XXV – Groddeck is one of those 'wild psychoanalysts' such as Reich and Ferenczi that I read a lot at one time (early sixties in Paris).

Wave XXVII – With Hokusai, not only the master of the floating world but the creator of great landscapes, there's no need of presentation. But, as with Bashô, I'll take the opportunity to quote the famous passage in which he describes his life's work, since it can stand as exemplary: 'At the age of six, I was seized with a strange mania to draw all kinds of things. At fifty, I had produced a great number of works of various kinds, but none completely satisfied me. The real work began for me when I was seventy. Now, at the age of seventy-five, I'm beginning to get a real feeling for nature. At eighty, I hope to have attained a certain power of intuition, and that it will develop till I'm ninety, so that at a hundred years of age I may possibly be able to say that my intuition was that of an authentic artist. And if I was ever lucky enough to live to a hundred-and-ten, I think a deep and living understanding of nature would radiate from every line I drew. I invite all those who'll live as long as me to see if I keep my word. Written at the age of seventy-five by me, once named Hokusai, the old man crazy with painting.' The name Hokusai, by the way, means 'Northern Study'. There are quite a few northern studies in this book.

Wave XXIX – Moscow-born Kandinsky was one of the founders of the Blue Rider School in Munich before settling in Paris. Yet another of those painters that meant a lot to me during the Glasgow years.

Wave XXX – The physicist referred to here is Lancelot Law Whyte, author of *The Unitary Principle in Physics and Biology*, *Aspects of Form* and *The Next Development in Man*.

Wave XXXI – The Japanese literatus is Nobuyuki Yuasa in his introduction to the English edition of Bashô's travel books.

Wave XXXIII – This is a translation by myself of the first of Rilke's *Duino Elegies*.

Wave XXXVI – The outlandish words here are Orkney Norn.

Wave XXXVIII – The 'Thomas of Cromarty' is of course Thomas Urquhart (1611–1660).

Wave XL – I'm giving here the Gaelic names (e.g. 'White Duncan of the Songs') of poets known more familiarly as Duncan MacIntyre (1724–1812), Alexander MacDonald (1700–1770) and John MacCodrum (1710–1796). The 'birlinn' is the famous *Birlinn Chlann Raghnaill* (Clan Ranald's Galley). As to *Oran na Muice*, 'The Song of the Sow', it's a scurrilous piece of inventive invective.

Wave XLI – Rabelais's words are: 'We can consider ourselves happy if we can always generously give to others', the best gift maybe to his mind (and mine) being 'a lovely book full of fine fat'.

Wave XLIV – An *'internationalgebildeter Mann'* (Saxl speaking of Scot) is a 'man of international education'. The Latin words I quote were all used by Scot, who loved subtle distinctions and precise definitions, in his astronomical work (in Toledo he translated Al-Bitrugi).

Wave XLVIII - The word 'harmony' as used by Heraclitus is so full of content and potentiality that I preferred to leave it here in the original Greek script.

BOOK IV

At the Sign of the Rosy Gull – Several months after writing this poem, I read in the *Birds of Scotland* by Baxter and Rintoul (Oliver & Boyd, Edinburgh, 1953): 'The only recorded occurrence of Ross's Gull in Scotland is that of an immature bird, which was caught off Whalsay, Shetland, on 28th April, 1936. It died within a few hours of capture.' April 28th, 1936 is my date of birth. I attach some importance to the coincidence for, as a Welsh poet said in similar circumstances: 'I'd be a bloody fool if I didn't.'

Letter from Harris – The lines quoted in section 2 are from one of the umpteen books on the geology of Scotland I have read over the years. I have a feeling this is from Fraser Darling. The works in section 5 were just picked at random (well, more or less) from Gaelic texts. *Faoileann* is a gull, *annlag mhara* is a sea-swallow, or storm petrel, *bòdhag* is a sea-lark, *breac-an-t-sil* is a wagtail. If I looked through the hundred notebooks stashed away in the hidey-holes of my library here on Brittany's north coast, I could, I think, get the source of the phrases quoted in section 2 about the practice of meditation, but I prefer just to meditate on them.

The Bodhi Notebook – Hakuin was a Zen master, one of the best. He was ten years old at the death of Bashô in 1695, and he died at the age of eighty-four. 'A wild tiger will never touch rotten meat', he said. It was because there was too much cultural rotten meat around that I went out, with Hakuin in my hand, into the cold. Hakuin is author of *A Quiet Night Talk on a Boat* (*Yasenkanwa*), and *The Teakettle* (*Orate Gama*). He was against 'sitting meditation' (*zazen*), and went in rather for what I'd call walking meditation. Painter, calligrapher and poet, he knew what he called 'the ecstasy of expression'. When his time had come, he lay down quietly to die. But at the very last moment, he let out a shout. He knew what he was doing.

River – In section 2, the man who couldn't walk along a river without tears in his eyes was Confucius. But I extrapolate, to all 'lovers of long thought', which is maybe, I submit, a better notion than 'philosopher'.

Scenes of a Floating World, Section 5 – 'Cold Mountain' is a reference to the Chinese poet Han Shan. See the note below to the poem 'Reading Han Shan in the Pyrenees'.

Mahamudra – Mahamudra ('the great seal', or 'the great gesture') is an important concept, and action, in tantric Buddhism. I went into this a lot in Paris – the book *Incandescent Limbo* is full of it. When I declared my intention to use this word as the title of a book of poems to be published by the Mercure de France, the literary director said I must be out of my mind, a book with a title like that would only get read in France by four immigrants from Tibet. I stuck to it. Even if readers just saw it as a big incomprehensible word, that would be fine – they would get into the 'incomprehensible' territory via the poems.

The Eight Eccentrics – The eight eccentrics (or immortals) are taoist figures. The ones I evoke most here are Lan Ts'ai-ho, Lü Tung Pin, Han Hsiang-tzu and Chang Kuo Lao. But Chung-li Ch'üan and Ts'ao Kuo Chiu are in the picture too. The word 'immortal' is written in Chinese with two pictographs meaning 'man' and 'mountain'.

BOOK V

In Aquitania – The memorial votive stone can still be seen, set in a wall, back of the church at Hasparren, in the Basque country.

The Master of the Labyrinth – I'm making no claim here to prehistorical reality. But who knows?

Valley of Birches – Two years after writing this poem, in the *Life of Milarepa* translated by Jacques Bacot, I came across this (it's the lama Yung-tön speaking to Milarepa): 'Go to the monastery of Tchro-ouo lung (Valley of Birches) [...] that's where Marpa lives, the man who knows all about the modern Tantra.'

Crow Meditation Text – The ultimate origin of this poem is a rookery in Fairlie, which I passed every day when I went to school. After that, there's a whole line of culture. Crow is an Amerindian trickster, cousin to the Kujkynnjaku who flaps his wings in Siberia. He's maybe a bit taoistic too. In the taoist tales, a crow resides in the sun, the place of plenitude and power. You find this solar crow also in Shinto, under the name of Yatagarasu. At the end of the eighteenth century, Chora published a collection of haiku entitled *The Whiteheaded Crow*. Compared to this high crow-line, Ted Hughes' crow sounds like a pathological punk, and that isn't the crow's fault: you see as big as your mind is. The anthropologist *enyerbado* (that is, 'who has smoked grass') is of course Carlos Castaneda, disciple of the Yaqui shaman Don Juan. This poem I dedicated to the pen I wrote it with, called Old Crow.

Mountain Study – The texts mentioned in section 5 are old Chinese texts often taken as calligraphy exercises by scholar-poets. Hsien-Yü Shu's copy of Ma Cheng-chün's 'Song of the Diaphanous Mirror' is considered a sublime masterpiece. Likewise Tung Ch'i-ch'ang's copy of Chou Tun-i's *Treatise on Understanding*. The text quoted in section 7 is Confucian, but I'm no longer sure from which book of the Confucian corpus.

Hölderlin in Bordeaux – After his studies at Tübingen, Hölderlin, in 1802, was a private tutor in Bordeaux. This Bordeaux period was a crucial one in his life. The phrases quoted are from his poem '*Brot und Wein*' ('Bread and Wine') and from letters sent to his friend Böhlendorff at that time. The thoughts I attribute to him are authentic, I maybe just radicalise them a bit, put my own edge to them.

Reading Han Shan in the Pyrenees – Han Shan was a Tang dynasty poet who chose as his poet's name 'Cold Mountain', from the place where he lived in the Tientai. Since the early sixties, there has been a Han Shan line in poetry, maybe even something like a 'Cold Mountain school'. It began with Burton Watson's translations of a hundred or so poems (1961). A few years later (1965) came Gary Snyder's *Cold Mountain*, a selection of twenty-four poems. Some time on, having already evoked the name of Han Shan in several texts, I received down there in the Pyrenees a French translation of the complete extant corpus. In my mind, there was a mountain triangle linking the Pyrenees to the Sierra Nevada of California (Snyder and I were in correspondence) and the mountains of Scotland. This wasn't a 'Sixties phenomenon' – it was the discovery of a high line that was due to last. In 2001, a book on mountains, to which I contributed, appeared in Edinburgh. Its title: *The Way to Cold Mountain*.

In the Sea and Pine Country – Geographically, we're in the pine-lands of the Landes area, in south-west France. Mentally, we're in a Kenzen meditation. Hakuin, as aforesaid, was against 'sitting meditation' (*zazen*), recommending rather movement. Whatever the method, the aim of meditation is to get to 'the other shore'. But if you get too much obsessed with the other shore, if you begin to capitalize on the notion, you'll never reach it, and will certainly never walk completely along it.

The Residence of Solitude and Light – In section 2, the poem by Gyôdai is quoted in Vol IV (Autumn–Winter) of R. H. Blyth's anthology *Haiku*. The work of Turner he refers to at the end of his commentary on the poem ('Blue smoke rising from unknown depths to unknown heights') is *The Crook of the Wye*. In section 5 ('Chao's discovery of Buddhism'), the reference is to a little known work, the *Chao Lun*, the 'treatise' of Seng-chao, fifth century. As to the Arabian and Indian grammarians mentioned (Khalil, Panini), it was one of their kind, Bhartrihari, who said that the study of grammar and the philosophy of language can lead to beatitude. Panini's grammar of Sanskrit goes back twenty-five centuries. Moving from grammar to yoga, Patanjali's *Yogadarsana* is a systematic presentation of yoga in four sections: Concentration, Practice, Power, Liberation. Painting is here represented by Sesshu Tôyô (1420–1506) – see the poem and the note on Sesshu in this book. Paul Valery's *long regard* ('long look') is that 'reward after the effort of thought' he speaks of in the poem *Le Cimetière marin* ('The Graveyard by the Sea').

BOOK VI

The Diamond Country – In the taoist book, *T'ai I Chin Hua Tsung Chih* (translated by Richard Whilhelm as 'the secret of the golden flower'), we read this: 'If you follow this method, you will find seminal water in abundance, the fire of the mind will kindle, and the earth of thought will condense and cristallize.' This process of cristallization (high energy poetics), is laid out with even more precision in the 'diamond philosophy' of certain tantric buddhist texts. In them, you meet the figure of the *vajrasattva*, the 'diamond being' who has reached, if not a total clarification of himself as body-speech-mind, at least a little light. The place where Siddhartha achieved his 'illumination' is called the *vajrasana* ('the diamond seat'), and in the *Surangamasutra*, we read: 'Wherever one arrives at illumination, that place is like a diamond.' More specifically, 'the diamond country' is the name of a *mandala* (Tucci translates: a psychocosmogram), the *vajradhatu-mandala*, inside which the adept tries to achieve enlightened consciouness. On the perimeter of this mandala, there are eight goddesses (i.e. inspirers, invitations to becoming), four of whom are abstract and four sensual. At the centre is the 'queen of the diamond country' (*vajradhatu-visvari*), or the 'girl of divine knowledge' (*jnanadakini*). This girl incarnates, embodies 'perfect wisdom' (*prajnaparamita*), which is often compared to a diamond. In the *Shrichakrasambhavatantra*, the yogin is advised to 'see in all that surrounds him the mandala of himself as *vajrasattva*'. And in the *Hwa Yen Sutra* (these notions are to be found in Sino-Japanese as well as in Indo-Tibetan Buddhism), we read: 'Only those who have diamond minds and who have realised the non-self can know the light.' Finally, let it be said that if it is good to have these notions in mind, it would be wrong to have them too much in mind: the esoteric (initiatic) content should never be allowed to overshadow or overweigh the direct sensation of the poem's reality. If you stick too close to the phenomenon (the world, or the language), you're going to be fooled, but if you stick too close to the emptiness (the abstract meaning, the diamond), you'll be suffering from religiosity sickness. If you're satisfied with 'poetry', you'll never get out on the road, never understand a thing, but if you get hung up on 'wisdom', it'll go dead on you.

Archaic Territory – Fa-hsien and Hsûan-tsang were Chinese buddhists (seventh century) who left for India via the Gobi desert in search of manuscripts. The best book on the cultural context and the travels themselves is probably René Grousset's *Sur les traces du Bouddha*. In it, he says of Hsûan-tsang (or Hiuan-tsang, depending on the transcriptions): 'In Hiuan-tsang there is not the slightest trace of exclusivism. And therein lies his strength. Many a monk was limited to the teachings of his sect, but not so Hiuan-tsang. His familiarity with the most widely differing schools made him unbeatable in argument. In the course of his metaphysical debates with the learned doctors of central Asia and India, he was always able to outdo them thanks to the weight of his erudition and the vivacity of his quotations.' Dutreil de Rhins and Frédéric Grenard were among the nineteenth and early twentieth century archaeologists who explored the sites in the Tarim Valley where so many ways of life and thought came together. As to the *Dhammapada* (the 'right path' in Pâli), it is an early Buddhist collection of 426 stanzas, famous both for its teaching and its literary value. That the text should have been written on birch bark may simply be due to the fact that birch was handy on the slopes of the Himalaya. But it may also be noted that in Indo-European languages, the words for 'tree' have a common root, and the original tree seems to have been a birch. The birch is to northern Eurasia what the bamboo is to cultures further south.

Winter Morning Train – What distinguishes the *Astâvakra gîtâ* from the better known *Bhagavad gîtâ* is that it shows no interest whatever in the idea of a personal God. It also livens up upanishadic vocabulary by the invention of new terms.

No Four-Star Hotel – I wouldn't want to turn this little midday-in-the-Midi poem into a heavy symbolical text (though rice, sardines and a tomato *could* signify, earth, sea and the sun...). But that red tomato reminds me of a phrase of Walt Whitman's. He said once that with a tomato in his hands he'd walk through the world and confound all the philosophers. Maybe that's what Husserl did with his phenomenology. Walt himself was on the right road (the good red road...), but he tended to talk too much. In haiku country, he would have founded the Red Tomato school, and done more walking than talking. A certain austerity, even asceticism, is essential to the haiku path and the diamond way – but with that austerity can go a lot of joyance and colour, sheer basic appetite.

Café du Midi – The epigraph of this poem ('Her body is fresh, subtle and delightful') is from a Provençal poem by Bernard de Ventadour.

Paradise Lodge – I later checked. The bird of this poem's print was *Ajaia ajaja*, of the stork family, now to be found mainly in the Florida everglades.

Equatorial – The birds I refer to here as albas are commonly known as fairy terns, a term which I loathe - too waltdisneyish. It's by going back to the scientific name *gygas alba* that I came to 'albas'. If anybody wants to see in this word a passing reference to Scotland (ancient and Gaelic name, Alba), I will not protest – I probably thought of it a little myself, hence the 'sk' of 'skim' and the use of 'wee'. The terns I call dark are usually called 'sooty'. As to 'saltheads', they are noddies – again a term I don't care for. I call these birds 'saltheads' because of the scattering of white on the tops of their heads, as also because of their skills in ocean fishing. The filao tree is also called casuarina, but, for several reasons, I prefer the former word. The Great Way is of course the Milky Way, without the dairy farm associations.

A Raw Blue Morning in Antwerp – Eloi Pruystinck, a slater to his trade, founded at the beginning of the sixteenth century, in Antwerp, a group known as the Loïsts. This group continued the tradition of the *Homines intelligentiae* and the Brothers of the Free Mind which had started up three centuries before. Anarchists, erotic mystics, libertine intellectuals, they were looked at sideways by the Papists, and condemned by the protestant Reformers. They were elsewhere, on other ground. After the visit that Eloi paid him in 1525, Luther wrote a letter to the 'Christians of Antwerp', telling them to have nothing to do with this *rumpelgeist*. Calvin for his part, in 1545, put out a pamphlet *Contre la secte phantastique et furieuse des libertins qui se nomment spirituels*. The Catholic mystic Suso (fourteenth century) had a dream in which he met up with a libertine intellectual and put a few questions to him: 'Where do you come from? Nowhere. What is your name? I am called nameless Nature. Where does your vision of things lead? Total freedom.' It's the old forces rising up against dogma, cults and structures. To be compared with taoist and tantric groups in the East.

Black Sea Letter – If there was a poet who fascinated me in my Latin studies at Glasgow, more than Horace, more than Virgil, more than Propertius, it was Ovid. His exile on the shores of the Black Sea was and is for me emblematic. I keep coming back to him. See 'Found on the Shore' and 'Ovid's Report' in this book.

Xenophanes of Kolophon – Not much is known about this presocratic philosopher, a contemporary of Pythagoras. He had apparently a keen mind, not without humour, and he did a lot of moving around. All we have of him are fragments: 'Seven decades have seen my unquiet thought wandering over the lands of Hellas.'

Saturday Night Whisky Talk – 'Ueno? Asakusa?' This is the last part of a haiku by Bashô. He's in his hut on the east bank of the Sumida River and, hearing bells ringing, wonders if they are those of Ueno or of Asakusa, two other quarters of Tokyo.

Wakan – Among the Indians of North America, *wakan* signifies 'sacred'. But it's not absolutely forbidden to read also into the title of this poem the word 'waken'.

The Anegada Passage – LIAT is the name of an airline company. In full: Leeward Islands Air Transport. In the Caribbean, they translate: Leave Island Any Time. Between Trinidad and Tortola (that was my beat, in fact they go from Caracas up to St Thomas), they do their best. I've flown with them many times, have cursed them many times, I still thank them.

Stones of the Cloudy Forest – Hsiang Pi Fêng had always wanted to go to Yellow Mountain, but it was only late on in life he could fulfil his desire, after spending long years 'ploughing with his tongue and eating rice-gruel', that is, earning his living by teaching. He was so delighted with his experience of the mountain that he felt he had to mark the event. So he began to go through all the books he could get his hands on, looking for poems or even just simple phrases concerning Yellow Mountain. Out of these poems and phrases he made an anthology.

North Road, Japan – The words *oshara shonara* are from a country Nô play danced in the Yamagata, north-west Japan. Like other words in such contexts, they mean nothing (they are probably, in origin, deformed Sanskrit), but they have an *aura*. In the economy of this poem, the words represent the language of something outside my habitual consciousness, and convey, to my ear, an impression of freshness and light, also, more abstractly, primalness, firstness (all those 'a's).

At Gwenved – 'Gwenved' is the name I gave to my house in Brittany. Literally 'the white country', it's a notion that is at the centre of Celtic culture, as ultimate place of concentration: *Gwenved* in Brythonic (Welsh, Breton), *Finn Mag* in Goedelic (Scots and Irish Gaelic). In Christian times, the word was used as a translation for 'paradise', but it is very much of this earth. I see it as a place of light and delight, the light, of course, not excluding darkness, the delight, not ignorant of fracture patterns.

Somewhere in Brittany – The words on the poster are a mixture of Breton and French. *Brezhoneg* is Breton for the Breton language. *A festnoz* is, literally, a 'night festival', and this one promised to last 'right till dawn' (*jusqu'à l'aube*).

BOOK VII

Isolario – All the notes on pilotage and on islands here were culled from old logbooks and nautical charts, Arabian, Chinese, Portuguese. I just re-wrote, re-arranged, composed. But the poem of course is also about something other than navigation.

The Western Gateways – It's in the prologue to his book, *Kora in Hell* (1920) that Williams speaks of that raw Atlantic beauty mentioned in section 7. Section 11 evokes symbolical itineraries in the Pyrenees going way back beyond the mediaeval pilgrimage to St

James of Compostella. Last point, need I insist that, if I depict in this poem the life of Basque whalers, I'm no partisan of whale-hunting today?

The Ocean Way – *Ozeanisches Gefühl* is that 'oceanic feeling' Freud mentions only in passing, but which Ferenczi developed in his *Thalassa*. Without something like it, identity is liable to be a shrunken, shrivelled, perverted thing (with only drugs to give it some kind of expansion). The phrase about 'whiteness' comes from Pound's *Cantos*. These are my Atlantic Cantos... In them, among other things, I gather together my affinities. Hence that trio, Pelagius, Scotus Erigena and Duns Scot. The first two have been mentioned elsewhere in these notes. As to Duns Scot (1266–1308), born near Edinburgh, working in Oxford, Paris and Cologne, he's the one Gerard Manley Hopkins called 'of reality the rarest-veinèd unraveller'. The last two lines welled up from my unconscious – they felt right, but sounded a bit strange. When I saw some time later the tantric buddhist mandala of the Dharmodaya, they seemed totally, indeed, uncannily justified. Finally, I'd like to make it clear that 'a head full of Irish whiskey' isn't to be taken quite literally, and that somebody else was driving the car.

The Armorican Manuscript – For this poem sequence, I had in mind a personage, a character, who would remain an undefined silhouette, but who would be trying to get his bearings in a new landscape, a new mindscape. The whole thing was to remain unfinished, open. I was thinking vaguely of *The Book of the Dean of Lismore* already mentioned in these notes: that manuscript containing extracts from the Ulster cycle, extracts from the Finn cycle and bits of poems by 'Blind Arthur' or 'Finlay the Red Bard' and others of their kind whose names are to be found only in the worn sheaf of pages that now lies in the National Library of Scotland. As for the *ora maritima* ('the shores of the sea') in section 3, it's the title of a long Latin poem by Rufius Festus Avienus (fourth century) which tells of an itinerary out of the Mediterranean up into the North Atlantic. My translation into French of this Latin text appeared as an artist's book in Paris (1994) under the title *Rivages d'Occident*. In section 4, the lines quoted are from an old Breton poem about the hero Bran, wounded at the battle of Kerloan. All the birds of the sea come to watch and keen over him, as well as an old rook and a young crow. It's not the warrior story that's interesting, it's the mytho-poetical background. In the Celtic languages, *bran* means not only crow, but sea-crow, that is, cormorant. The reference to Megara in section 5 comes from Pausonias: in his description of Greece, *Hellados periegesis* (second century AD) he speaks of the existence, on the coast of Megara, of a promontory dedicated to the goddess Athena – she was there in the form of a cormorant. All this extends the network of image while pulling the text together tighter (but not *too* tight). I like the juxtaposition of Celtic and Greek. Celtic monks would often talk Greek together, to annoy the Roman occupiers by showing them they were better educated and more literate than the Romans. Marban the hermit evoked in section 6 was the brother of Guaire, king of Connaught (seventh century). The lines I quote are from a poem he's supposed to have composed when his brother came to persuade him to quit his hermitage and go into politics. The old Gaelic poem begins thus: *Ata varboth dam i caill* ('I have a shelter in the woods'). After thirty-two stanzas, the king agreed that Marban was right. In section 8, the Latin terms are from John Erigena's *Periphyseon* and are about the movement of the mind from the visible to the invisible. What I like about Erigena is the combination of maximal knowledge, vigour of thought, live language and powerful poetics – with that you're really going places, not just marking time. The point of departure for the poem in section 10 was a single word *brumennin* in the old Breton ballad *Droukkinnig Nevenoiou*. I dropped all the story and concentrated on topography, which is the general tendency of my work: from history to geography and from geography to... something else. The poem in section 12 has its source in the old Breton ballads about Merlin, in particular *Marzhin Divinour* ('Merlin the Soothsayer'). The figure of Iscolan (or Yscolan, Skolan, Skolvan, according to the manuscripts) is from an old ballad situated on the border between paganism and Christianity. The 'shanty song' of section 17 I wrote myself – I was getting so much into the swing of the tradition that it came quite naturally. All in all, this sequence was an attempt to get into the depths of Breton culture while exploring further my own territory. That's what I do all along.

Broken Ode to White Brittany – 'White Brittany' has nothing to do with the colour symbolism of the French Revolution: white (royalist), blue (republican). I also speak of 'blue Brittany'. Blue for me is an aspect of white. White is uninscribed – and with that in mind, I sometimes use Armorica instead of the connotated Brittany (similarly, Alba for Scotland). The poem is an exploration of topography, the sketching out of a cartography, and the outline of a poetics.

The House at the Head of the Tide – Oceanic mandala ... The 'white field' actually exists, right next to my place in Brittany ('objective chance' was the name André Breton gave to this kind of coincidence). 'Peace in the breakers' is a little salutation in the bygoing to another French-language poet I feel close to, Henri Michaux. The lines quoted about 'still moving' are from T. S. Eliot's *Four Quartets* – I'm moving here to a fifth. The 'one who has thought his way through the thicket' is Martin Heidegger (in his best texts). There's a cluster of monastic vocabulary at one point in this poem: *scriptorium* (where texts were written), *candida casa* (Ninian's monastery in the south-west of Scotland) and *altus prosator* ('high proser' – that is, roughly, poet). But the general context is not christic, it is chaoticist (order in disorder, anarchic coherence).

Ovid's Report – While having in mind Ovid's exile on the Black Sea and texts such as the *Halieutica* attributed to him at that time and place, I'm pushing him farther than he ever went. Again, this isn't fiction, it's extension. I'm gathering here all my affinities into one great field.

Brandan's Last Voyage – The passage quoted at the beginning of this poem is from a thirteenth century French manuscript, *L'Image du Monde*, which contains the French translation of a Latin text, *Navigatio Sancti Brandani*, a copy of which was conserved in an abbey of 'black monks' in Lorraine. The 'Navigation of St Brandan' relates the sea-travels of this fifth century monk between Ireland and the Azores, with particular concentrations on the Western Isles of Scotland and the Breton coast (where Brandan paid a visit to St Malo). In the name Brandan, there is the word '*bran*', meaning 'crow', and Bran is also the name of a Celtic hero to whom several poems are dedicated, one of which is quoted in section 2. There never was a 'last voyage' by Brandan. I just wanted to make it for him, with him.

Labrador – The protagonist of this poem is one of those Scandinavian sea-travellers like Leif Ericson or Thorfinn Karlsefni who were active around the tenth century, and who touched on American shores: Helluland (the land of the flat stones), Markland (the land of forests), Vinland (the grasslands). My character is true to type, but a little extended and developed. He uses on occasion the complex metaphor (*kenning*) particular to Nordic poetry: 'storm of words' (war), 'sky of sands' (sea), and so on, but he moves away beyond the wordy complications some skalds went in for when they were playing to the gallery.

Logos Amerikanos – In this panorama of approaches to America, attempts to get at 'the logic of the land', after the cartographer Juan de la Cosa working at his 'painting of the earth', you have Samuel de Champlain whose reports *Of Savages* and *The Travels* appeared in the early seventeenth century. In section 4, what is evoked is the exploration by Lewis and Clark (1804–1806) of the wilderness lying between the Mississippi and the Pacific (they went along the Columbia, the Yellowstone, the Missouri, the White River, taking copious notes), as well as Meriwether Lewis's last days. Dupaix's huge Mexican volume I consulted in Paris. As to Audubon, born in Santo Domingo, he studied painting in Paris before making for America in 1803. His book, *The Birds of America* (435 great plates) came out from Edinburgh around 1830. The man talking in section 7 is Henry Dana (*Two years before the Mast*). In section 8, it's Knud Rasmussen (*From Greenland to the Pacific*). For years I ran a seminar in Paris on 'Approaches to America' using all this material, and a lot more like it. But the ultimate statement is the poem, taking the whole corpus of information and conjecture into another dimension.

The Winter Ceremony – At his death in 1943, the ethnologist Franz Boas left an unfinished study on the peoples of the North-West Pacific: *Kwakiutl Ethnography*. It's one of the most beautiful ethnographic texts I know of. More than half of the manuscript is devoted to a shamanist festival, 'The Winter Ceremony'. There on the Breton coast, it was the winter of 1984.

Melville at Arrowhead – In a fine essay on Melville, Jean Giono speaks of minds that devote all their efforts to some 'monstrous' object. This pursuit implies all kinds of underground work, done in solitude and silence, as well as various kinds of spatial movement.

All the world often sees, says Giono, is the 'awesome whiteness' of a shipwreck or a transcendence.

The Chaoticist Manifesto – This wild piece came to me largely when I was walking the coast between Trébeurden and Île-Grande. As well as being a hymn to chaoticism, it's a coastal colloquium in which Pelagius and John Scot Erigena rub shoulders with Martin Heidegger (*'Ereignis'*, *'Anfang'* belong to his vocabulary), while a Chinese taoist, an adept of *fengshui* ('wind and water' practice), also wanders about in the vicinity.

First Colloquium of the Gull Academy – In 'Crow Meditation Text' (see section V of this book, *Mountain Meditations*), I say: 'I once thought of founding an Academy of Gulls'. Well, here it is.

Letter from the Isles of America – My own physical approaches to North America have been mainly from the north (Labrador, Quebec, Maine) and the south (the Antillean islands), as in this poem, and in several others in the book. All the places mentioned in this particular poem are on Martinique.

Finisterra – Yaudet stands on a headland overlooking the mouth of the Léguer that runs through Lannion on the north coast of Brittany. Pyrrho of Elis (365–275 BC) tried his hand first at painting, then studied under Euclid of Megara, then travelled with Alexander into Asia. The mental attitude resulting was scepticism. I studied scepticism a lot at one time, mainly in the works of Sextus Empiricus. There's a very fine territory lying between scepticism and phenomenology.

Late August on the Coast – *Niflheim* ('house of mist') is an area in the Scandinavian dream-world. My place in Brittany sometimes feels like it. The Japanese prints mentioned are by Hiroshige. As with other poems in this seventh and final book, I'm gathering together all my elective affinities. But it's the birds that get the last word: invocations to open world.